# THE
# GREAT CASTLES
## OF BRITAIN & IRELAND

## LISE HULL

*Photography by*

## STEPHEN WHITEHORNE

First published in 2005 by New Holland Publishers (UK) Ltd
London • Cape Town • Sydney • Auckland

www.newhollandpublishers.com

Garfield House, 86–88 Edgware Road, London W2 2EA, United Kingdom

80 McKenzie Street, Cape Town 8001, South Africa

14 Aquatic Drive, Frenchs Forest, NSW 2086, Australia

218 Lake Road, Northcote, Auckland, New Zealand

10 9 8 7 6 5 4 3 2 1

ISBN  1 84330 898 3

Publishing Manager: Jo Hemmings
Senior Editor: Kate Michell
Assistant Editor: Rose Hudson
Cover Design and Design: Alan Marshall
Cartography: William Smuts
Indexer: Dorothy Frame
Production: Joan Woodroffe

Reproduction by Pica Digital Pte Ltd, Singapore
Printed and bound in Singapore by Tien Wah Press (Pte) Ltd

Photographs appearing on the cover and prelim pages are as follows:
Front cover: Bodiam Castle, England.
Back cover: (top left) Arundel Castle, England; (Top right) Glamis Castle,
Scotland; (bottom left) Bodiam Castle, England; (bottom right) Berkeley
Castle, England.
Front flap: Bunratty Castle, Ireland.
Back flap: Eilean Donan Castle, Scotland.
Spine: Trim Castle, Ireland.
Page 1: Caerlaverock Castle, Scotland.
Right: Beaumaris Castle, Wales.
Page 4: (top) Threave Castle, Scotland; (middle) Kenilworth Castle,
England; (bottom) Caerlaverock Castle, Scotland.
Page 5: Rochester Castle, England.
Page 160: Corfe Castle, England.

# CONTENTS

Introduction                           6

⛉ GREAT CASTLES                      16
   OF ENGLAND

Carlisle Castle                       18
Bamburgh Castle                       20
Alnwick Castle                        22
Warkworth Castle                      25
Conisbrough Castle                    27
Castle Rising                         29
Kenilworth Castle                     31
Warwick Castle                        34
Goodrich Castle                       37
Berkeley Castle                       40
Windsor Castle                        43
Tower of London                       46
Rochester Castle                      50
Dover Castle                          52
Bodiam Castle                         56
Arundel Castle                        59
Corfe Castle                          61
Restormel Castle                      64

🌿 GREAT CASTLES                      66
   OF SCOTLAND

Threave Castle                        68
Caerlaverock Castle                   71
Hermitage Castle                      74
Edinburgh Castle                      77
Stirling Castle                       79
Bothwell Castle                       82
Rothesay Castle                       84
Glamis Castle                         86
Dunnottar Castle                      88

Urquhart Castle                90

Eilean Donan Castle            92

Dunvegan Castle                95

GREAT CASTLES              98
OF WALES

White Castle                  100

Raglan Castle                 103

Chepstow Castle               106

Caerphilly Castle             110

Kidwelly Castle               114

Pembroke Castle               116

Harlech Castle                119

Dolwyddelan Castle            122

Caernarfon Castle             124

Beaumaris Castle              128

Conwy Castle                  130

Rhuddlan Castle               133

GREAT CASTLES              136
OF IRELAND

Carrickfergus Castle          138

Roscommon Castle              140

Trim Castle                   142

Bunratty Castle               145

Limerick Castle               147

Rock of Cashel                149

Kilkenny Castle               152

Cahir Castle                  154

Contact Details               156

Glossary & Further Reading    157

Index                         158

Acknowledgements              160

# INTRODUCTION

*Thanks to theme parks, movies and video games, people around the world believe real castles resemble Mad Ludwig's Neuschwanstein in Bavaria or Disney's Cinderella Castle. Yet both structures, glorious as they may be, are most accurately labelled 'palaces' or even 'fantasy residences'. Simply adorning a stately home with a regal name that includes the word 'castle' gives the impression that one's home is a castle in the most authentic sense of the word. However, although many owners built their grand residences on a monumental scale, fitted the towered halls with evenly spaced battlements and erected elaborate gatehouses to impress their friends and passers-by, such structures are merely shams. They may look like castles, but their owners never intended them to act as military strongholds. In fact, in Britain castles gave way to artillery fortresses and palatial residences as social and cultural values changed during the reigns of Henry VIII (1509–47) and Elizabeth I (1558–1603), and as the technology and tactics of warfare shifted to cannons and the battlefield.*

**What is a Castle?**

Simply put, a real castle is a fortified military residence. As such, it housed a lord and his family and functioned in a military capacity at the same time, dominating an area, subjugating the local population and garrisoning a group of

ABOVE: *A decorative duo of machicolations opens outwards over Cahir Castle's gate passage, which is guarded by a portcullis. The defensive projections allowed soldiers in the chamber overhead to drop missiles and boiling water onto attackers.*

RIGHT: *Initially defended with timber ramparts and crowned with a timber tower, the classic motte-and-bailey castle featured the motte, a mound raised with human labour, and at least one enclosure, the bailey, created with earthen embankments (after Scotland's Duffus Castle).*

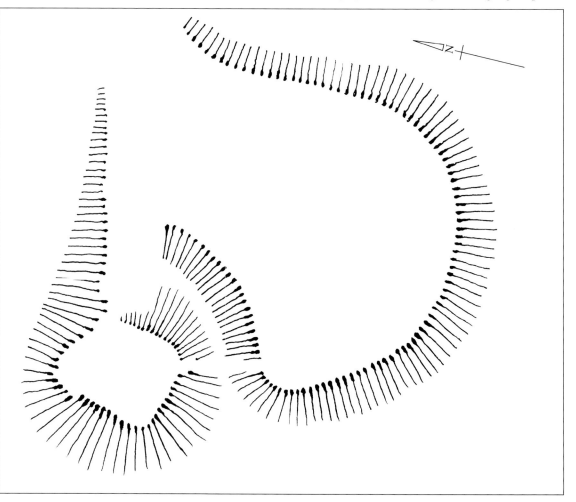

soldiers as required. In most cases, owners only spent a portion of each year at their castles, administering justice, entertaining dignitaries and handling whatever tasks came their way. These men often acted as mini-kings; but, ultimately, they owed allegiance to the monarch who required them to pay a 'knight's fee' for the right to maintain the castle and live off the local economy. Their castles emphasized power and showcased wealth, but also provided the basic necessities of daily life.

Few medieval castles actually contained all the features we normally identify with the castles of our imaginations. Most were much simpler structures, built to meet the military requirements and residential preferences of their owners. Most castle-builders, lords and men of lesser nobility, had limited resources to fund the construction of a castle. Accordingly, these limitations restricted the scope of the building programme. Only the most prosperous men could afford to raise powerful fortresses like Alnwick in Northumberland (see pages 22–4) or Warwick in the Midlands (see pages 34–6). Nonetheless, whether large or

small, stone or timber, castles shared the same dual purpose – they all provided a lord with a defended residence.

## Types of Castle

Castles in Britain and Ireland may broadly be classified as earth-and-timber castles (mottes and ringworks), stone-enclosure castles, concentric castles, quadrangular castles or tower houses. Many originated as earth-and-timber fortifications and never acquired stone structures. Some timber castles, re-fortified with masonry defences and permanent buildings, for example Windsor (see pages 43–5), developed into stone-enclosure castles. Other castles began as simple stone-enclosure castles, but developed into complex concentric fortresses, while late in the history of castle-building, straightforward quadrangular designs and tower houses spread throughout the landscape.

## Norman Development

Even before conquering the Saxons in 1066, Duke William of Normandy (1027–87) began his invasion of England by erecting two earth-

ABOVE: *The substantial motte known as Tomen Castell peeks through a tree-laden canopy at the edge of forest lands near the stone castle at Dolwyddelan in Wales. Scores of these earth-and-timber castles dot the countryside of Britain and Ireland.*

RIGHT: *Castle Rising's castle in England exemplifies the ringwork and bailey castle. Here, the huge central ringwork contains several stone structures, including an outstanding Norman keep. To either side, rectangular baileys provided added protection.*

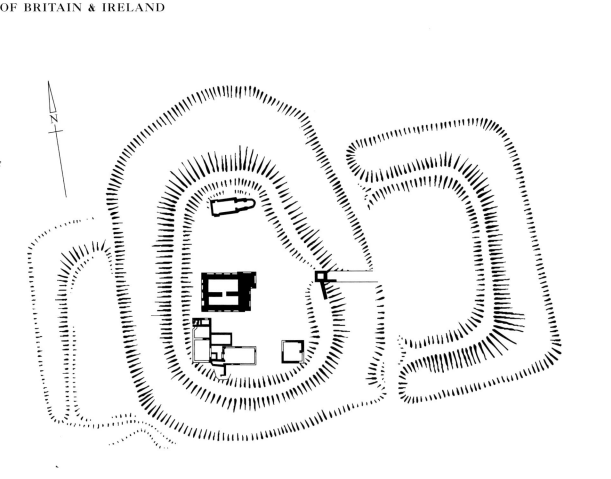

BELOW: *Cut by the remains of the crumbling gatehouse, the massive embankments at Castle Rising surround the Norman great keep, which dominates the inner bailey. Enclosed on either side by two more baileys, the ringwork castle is one of the largest and most complex of its kind.*

and-timber castles. One was at Pevensey in Sussex, where the Norman fleet had landed; the other was some distance away at Hastings. Here, William erected a motte castle on a craggy hilltop overlooking the now sprawling town. In a matter of days, the Norman army defeated the Saxons and killed their king, Harold II, and at Christmas their leader became William I, the first Norman king of England. Shortly afterwards, he ordered the construction of an

earth-and-timber castle at Dover and a series of castles to ring his capital city, London. William clearly recognized the value of erecting castles as power bases from which to subjugate a population and rule a kingdom. During the two decades of his reign, scores of castles appeared in the countryside.

Consider what William needed from a castle – a good vantage point, sound defences, the ability to dominate an area and an easy-to-build, cost-effective design. Earth-and-timber castles met those criteria. Made of local material and requiring little skill to construct, the man-made mounds and earthwork enclosures provided the ideal way to effect a quick conquest.

During the reign of William I's predecessor, Edward the Confessor (1042–66), the Saxons had already erected a few timber castles at Hereford, Ewyas Harold and Richard's Castle, and possibly another at Clavering in Essex. Favouring life in the Norman courts, Edward the Confessor and his Anglo-Saxon subjects apparently experimented with this innovative French castle design. However, the responsibility for erecting hundreds of earth-and-timber castles throughout England and Wales falls directly on the shoulders of William the Conqueror and his men. In the 12th century, when the Normans expanded into Scotland and Ireland, they also built earth-and-timber castles to dominate their new territories.

The Normans erected two different yet similar types of earth-and-timber castle: mottes and ringworks. By far the more common of the two, the motte consisted of a mound formed by heaping up the earth excavated from what became the encircling ditch. Some mottes reached an incredible 80–100 feet (24.4–30.5 metres) in height and measured twice that in basal diameter. Many were created by modifying rocky outcrops or piling up chalky rubble and then packing earth over the mounds. Topped with a wooden or stone tower, which was known as a shell keep, the steep-sided motte served both a military and a residential role, afforded elevated protection for inhabitants and allowed guards to observe activity in the area.

Most motte castles were protected with at least one bailey, a large area of land enclosed by earthen embankments topped with timber palisades. A hive of activity, the noisy bailey teemed with soldiers, labourers, craftsmen, servants completing daily household chores and livestock wandering freely about. The bailey also housed an assortment of timber structures, such as the hall, kitchen or stables. Later owners often replaced the timber defences with masonry curtain walls to strengthen their castles against fire, damp and rot. Many of these sites, including England's Warwick and Arundel (see pages 59–60), survived as substantial stone-enclosure castles.

Ringwork castles also appeared in Britain immediately after the Conquest. Less common than motte castles, ringworks consisted of a mound, the rim of which was encircled with earthen banks that were then topped with timber palisades. However, unlike the flat-topped motte, the summit of the suitably named

ringwork was scooped out, so that the outer perimeter stood taller than the centre of the mound. The ringwork at Castle Rising Castle in Norfolk (see pages 29–30) is one of England's finest examples of this sort of structure.

## Stone-Enclosure Castles

Logically, one would expect castles to evolve from the simplest fortifications to the most complex fortresses; however, this did not happen in Britain and Ireland. Rather, both earth-and-timber and stone castles emerged in the countryside in the decades immediately after the Norman Conquest. Indeed, kings and lords continued to construct both castle types for several centuries.

No two stone-enclosure castles followed the same standard design nor had the same shape.

ABOVE: *Strategically placed at intervals along the curtain wall, the set of round and rectangular towers at Limerick made the stone-enclosure castle virtually invulnerable to waterborne assaults.*

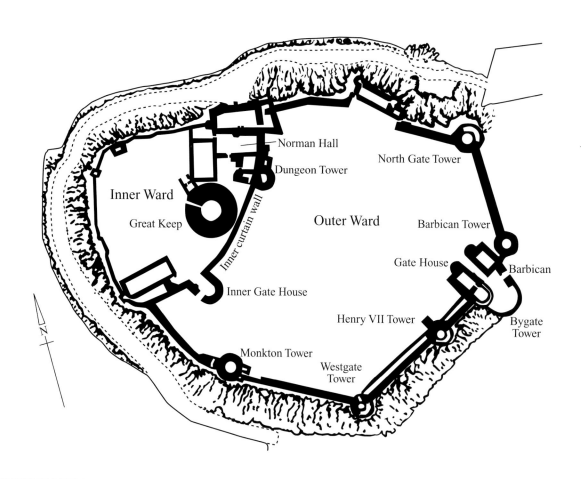

Norman Hall

North Gate Tower

Dungeon Tower

Inner Ward

Great Keep

Outer Ward

Barbican Tower

Inner curtain wall

Gate House

Barbican

Inner Gate House

Henry VII Tower

Bygate
Tower

Monkton Tower

Westgate
Tower

N

Many earthwork fortifications, including the Tower of London (see pages 46–9), Castle Rising Castle and Limerick Castle (see pages 147–8), began as primitive earth-and-timber castles, and became the realm's mightiest strongholds with the addition of masonry walls. Others, for example Chepstow Castle (see pages 106–109) on the southern border separating Wales and England, originated as masonry fortresses. Dating to 1067, Chepstow's massive hall-keep, which centres the site, is believed to be Britain's oldest surviving secular stone building.

Most commonly, stone-enclosure castles featured reasonably strong stone curtain walls, which enclosed both the inner and outer baileys. Equipped with regularly spaced mural towers, the thick walls girdled vital residential and military structures, and also the castle's inhabitants. Like their earth-and-timber counterparts, stone-enclosure castles dominated, subjugated and intimidated the local populace. They also impressed rival lords. Some, such as Caerlaverock (see pages 71–3), were triangular. Others, like the oblong castles at Arundel and Warwick, had walled baileys creating defensive zones on either side of a central mound or great tower. Some castles, for example Rochester (see pages 50–51) and Dover (see pages 52–5), had keeps, which were self-sufficient towers able to defend themselves during a siege. Others, for example Framlingham in Norfolk, did not.

## Concentric Castles

Concentric castles represent the pinnacle of castle-building, not only in the British Isles, but in Europe and the Holy Land as well. During the 13th century, the concentric plan served a surprisingly simple purpose. By then, military leaders had identified the need to concentrate their castle's firepower at a target and to interfere with the destructive pounding of increasingly sophisticated siege engines. The solution was a series of embedded defences, whereby outer towers and gatehouses stood lower than towers and gatehouses closer to the centre. The 'walls-within-walls' design permitted defenders to fire upon the enemy from both levels simultaneously while avoiding their own men. The confined landfall between the embedded walls formed an unfamiliar and cramped space that confused invaders. If the enemy managed to breach the exterior wall, soldiers on top of the

ABOVE: *Built in the 13th century, Bamburgh's twin-turretted gatehouse provided a stop-gap for visitors wanting entry into the enclosure castle's three baileys. Located at the easternmost tip of the castle, the gatehouse had features consistent with the standard medieval barbican.*

LEFT: *Situated alongside the entrance into the well, Kenilworth keep's unusual arrow-slit window features splayed sides and steps climbing to the opening.*

RIGHT: *The archetypal concentric castle, Caerphilly in Wales, features a walls-within-walls design where outer defences, like the gatehouses, stand lower than their counterparts closer to the centre of the castle.*

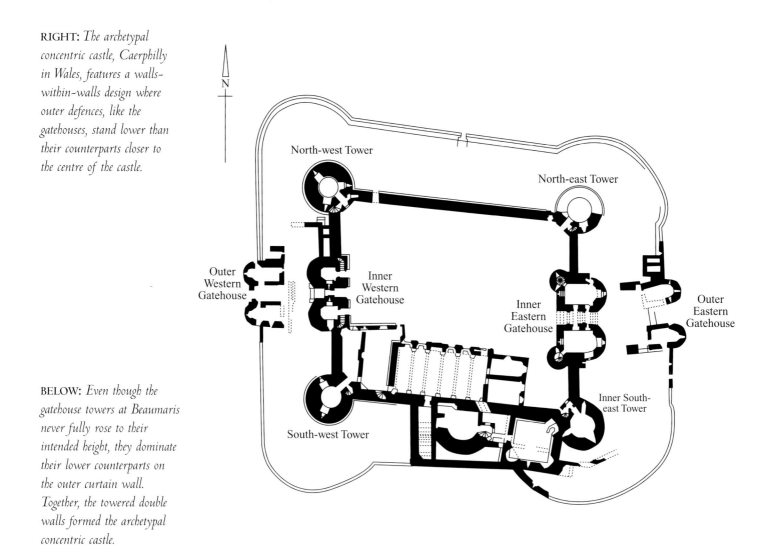

N

North-west Tower

North-east Tower

Outer
Western
Gatehouse

Inner
Western
Gatehouse

Inner
Eastern
Gatehouse

Outer
Eastern
Gatehouse

Inner South-
east Tower

South-west Tower

BELOW: *Even though the gatehouse towers at Beaumaris never fully rose to their intended height, they dominate their lower counterparts on the outer curtain wall. Together, the towered double walls formed the archetypal concentric castle.*

inner wall could direct all their firepower towards the exposed, disorganized attackers.

Some stone-enclosure castles, such as the Tower of London and the Welsh fortress of Kidwelly (see pages 114–5), acquired the concentric design over time, as owners constructed stronger structures to bolster their defensive capabilities. Others originated as concentric castles and flourished during the late 13th century. In 1267, Gilbert de Clare, Earl of Gloucester (1243–95), intermingled massive stone and lake-like water defences to create the archetypal concentric fortress at Caerphilly (see pages 110–13). Fifteen years later, de Clare's king, Edward I (1272–1307), began his great concentric masterpieces, Harlech Castle (see pages 119–21) and Beaumaris Castle (see pages 128–9), which UNESCO has designated as World Heritage Sites.

## Quadrangular Castles

In time, complexity gave way to simplicity and symmetry. As its name implies, the quadrangular castle had four sides. Most were arranged in the shape of a square and enclosed an inner courtyard. At fortresses such as Roscommon Castle (see pages 140–41), a gatehouse dominated at least one side and towers defended each corner. Residential chambers, the hall block and a chapel lined interior walls and filled the towers. Moats surrounded many quadrangular castles, as at Bodiam (see pages 56–8), arguably the best – and certainly the most photographed – example of its kind.

## Tower Houses

Comprised of a series of single-chambered storeys, which were stacked vertically one upon the other, the Scottish tower house developed as a response to the need for protection from sudden, brief attack rather than to withstand prolonged sieges. Tower houses emerged in the

RIGHT: *The well-proportioned quadrangular castle at Bodiam in England typifies the late phase of castle building in Britain, when symmetry and image became as important as defensive might.*

BELOW: *The classic quadrangular castle, majestic Bodiam exudes symmetry, strength and grace as it rises from the depths of the surrounding moat.*

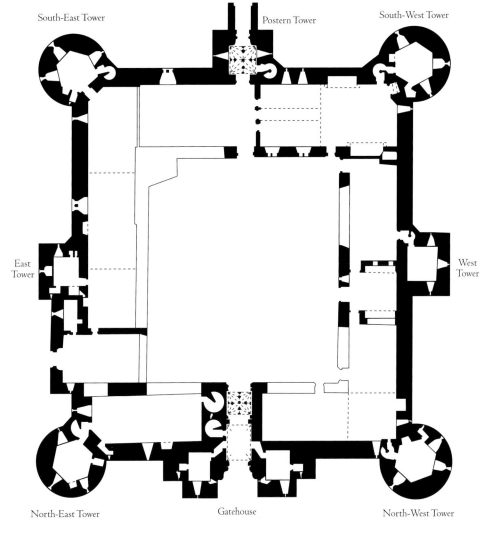

South-East Tower

Postern Tower

South-West Tower

East Tower

West Tower

North-East Tower

Gatehouse

North-West Tower

**ABOVE:** *Commanding sweeping vistas of Loch Ness, the tower house at Urquhart Castle was ideally poised to guard Scotland's Great Glen, a natural, water-filled fault line that bisects the Highlands.*

wake of the Wars of Independence, when Scotland was still riddled with uncertainty, clans continued to fight each other, and small bands of marauders, sometimes known as Border Reivers, plundered the countryside.

Often associated with walled enclosures known as barmkins, tower houses rose 40–80 feet (12.2–24.4 metres) high and had at least three levels. With thick walls, first-floor entrances barred with iron grates and few windows, the entire focus was on defence. Each level served a single function: a storage area filled the ground floor; the first floor held the hall or kitchen; and residential chambers occupied the uppermost levels.

The L-plan tower house, which had a smaller wing constructed at a right angle to the main tower, developed in the late 14th century to provide additional living space and a modicum of comfort in the otherwise stark structures. The addition of two wings projecting from corners on the same side of the main tower

created a U-shaped plan. The Z-plan tower house sported offsetting wings jutting out from opposite ends of the main rectangular tower, which augmented the castle's defensive capacity. Once extra wings became routine additions, the central tower could hold more lavish living quarters, and rooms like the kitchen, hall and chapel shifted to the annexes. While most tower houses were self-sufficient strongholds, some stood within the walls of stone-enclosure castles, including Dunnottar (see pages 88–9), Urquhart (see pages 90–91) and even Edinburgh Castle (see pages 77–8), where David II (1329–71) built an L-shaped tower house to replace a royal residence destroyed during the Wars of Independence.

In the late 17th century, grand baronial residences emphasizing comfort over defence began to replace the Scottish tower house. Many, for example Threave Castle (see pages 68–70), fell into ruin. At others, like Glamis (see pages 86–7) and Dunvegan (see pages

## Transcending Time

The great castles of Britain and Ireland testify to changing times, changing values and the changes forged by conquest and migration. They survive in towns and on hilltops, in cities and on farmland. Whether ruined or occupied, built from earth and timber or rubble, each offers a unique connection to real people, people who lived, laboured and died in their shadow. Exploring the great castles of Britain and Ireland allows us to reconnect physically with the past, and to gain insight into the present. Majestic monuments and humble mounds, each played a role not only in influencing the history of Britain and Ireland, but also in shaping world history. That they survive is a tribute to the men who designed and built them and also to the hardiness and fortitude of the men, women and children who occupied them and the peasantry who supported them. They also reflect the magnitude of the threat posed by local populations intent on regaining their freedom.

Even in ruin, castles exude a timelessness that inspires awe and binds past and present. The stones and earthen mounds truly have their own stories to tell. If we listen, we will discover not only the heritage of Britain and Ireland, but also the lessons of history.

*BELOW: Typical Scottish tower houses consisted of one of three basic designs, the simple rectangular plan, the L-plan and the Z-plan. Built to resist sudden attacks, tower houses were modest in comparison to their grander counterparts, but performed the dual functions of all true castles: they were fortified residences built for men of at least moderate status.*

95–7), flamboyant architectural styles engulfed the simpler medieval strongholds. The tower house now survives as part of the inner core of such structures.

Irish tower houses developed in the early 15th century to defend against sudden attacks. Ranging from three to six storeys high, their distinctive top levels featured stepped battlements and a double-gabled roof, which held the attic. Those fitted with an extra corner turret resembled Scotland's L-plan tower house, while those having turrets at opposite ends resembled the Z-plan tower house.

Much like the Scottish tower house in design and function, the pele tower appeared in northern England to defend against assaults by small raiding parties. Smaller than the average tower house, their walls averaged 3–4 feet (0.9–1.2 metres) in thickness. Many featured a barmkin. At one time, Northumberland supported 200 pele towers, while in Cumberland and Westmoreland, 90 peles were built.

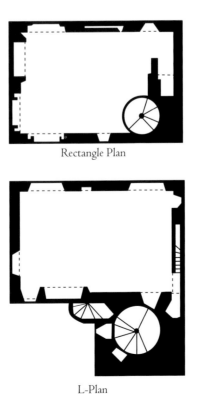

Rectangle Plan

L-Plan

Z-Plan

# GREAT CASTLES OF
# ✠ ENGLAND

When Duke William of Normandy landed on England's southern
shores in 1066, he immediately erected an earthwork castle
inside the old Roman fort at Pevensey in Sussex. After
defeating Harold II, William promptly built another
castle, this time overlooking Dover's white cliffs
and the English Channel across which enemies
might sail. In time, many of the Conqueror's
simple but powerful earth-and-timber strongholds metamorphosed into important buildings,
such as the Tower of London, while others, like
Restormel in Cornwall, remained essentially
unchanged. Farther north, the Conqueror's men
constructed an array of fortresses. Many, such as
Berkeley and Warwick, began as earth-and-timber
castles, but developed into the highly defended yet
stately residences of England's most influential
personalities. Still others — as with the awe-
inspiring ruins of King John's beloved Corfe
Castle and the majestic Percy strongholds at
Arundel, Warkworth and Bamburgh — form
the stuff of legends. Right across the country,
England's castles steadfastly display the
power, status and ambitions of
the men and women who
shaped the landscape
and the course
of history.

## HISTORY

**1st to 4th centuries AD** – Romans base a garrison at fort known as Luguvalium.

**1092** – William II erects earth-and-timber castle.

**1122** – Henry I begins stone keep and town defences.

**1136** – King Stephen surrenders castle to the Scottish King David I.

**1153** – David I dies at the castle.

**1157** – Henry II forces Scots to retreat; extends castle defences.

**1173** – The Scottish monarch, William the Lion, besieges castle for three months.

**1216** – Alexander II, King of the Scots, captures castle and destroys keep; castle used as barons' headquarters against King John.

**1295** – Edward I grants custody of castle to Robert the Bruce, Lord of Annandale.

**1296** – John Comyn and Scots attack castle.

**1306–7** – Edward I stages invasion of southern Scotland from castle.

**1315** – Robert the Bruce attacks, but bad weather forces retreat.

**1323** – Edward II executes Andrew de Harcla, Earl of Carlisle, for conspiring with Robert the Bruce against English.

**1378–83** – Richard II spends £500 to rebuild castle; used as residence for Warden of the March.

**1461** – Lancastrians and Scots besiege castle.

**1483** – Richard III builds first gun-tower.

**1541** – Henry VIII adds Half-Moon Battery.

**1547** – Magazine explodes, breaching keep walls.

**1568** – Prison for Mary, Queen of Scots after her defeat at the Battle of Langside.

**1645** – Royalist garrison surrenders after siege lasting eight months; Covenanters repair defences.

**1745** – Jacobites led by Bonnie Prince Charlie seize castle in six days; Duke of Cumberland forces their surrender.

**1959** – Military occupation of Carlisle ceases.

# Carlisle Castle

Located at the westernmost end of the Stanegate, which was the Roman roadway that crossed northern England, the Cumbrian city of Carlisle has long been valued for its strategic value. In 1092, some 500 years after the Romans abandoned the post, the Normans established themselves at the site, which had been in Scottish hands since 1068. Recognizing the potency of the location – Scotland is a mere 10 miles (16km) away and the site stands on a bluff overlooking the River Eden – Carlisle was deemed the ideal place to erect a castle.

### Carlisle Through the Centuries

In the Middle Ages, Carlisle became a key forward outpost for England's monarchs during their long struggle against the Scots. Later, the castle became a depot for arms and ammunition and a barracks for the military, which remained there throughout the Second World War (1939–45). Even though extensive modifications over the centuries have transformed the original stronghold into a powerful artillery fortress, the layout of the castle remains true to its medieval origins. A masonry cross-wall and ditch separate the site into inner and outer

**ABOVE:** *Royal heraldic emblems, such as this one dating to the reign of Queen Elizabeth I, adorn the castle walls.*

**LEFT:** *Mary, Queen of Scots would have seen a similar view as this from her chamber in the tower that served as her prison. Across the courtyard, the massive great keep was an ominous vision*

**PREVIOUS PAGE:** *Norman construction in all its glory. Crowning the huge motte, Arundel Castle's battlemented great keep displays the power and defensive might that caused attackers to pause before its walls.*

baileys, and a stone curtain wall frames the entire complex. A single gateway breached the wall's southern side, so that visitors from the city could gain entry to the castle. All in all, Carlisle is an outstanding example of a stone-enclosure castle.

As early as the 12th century, Henry I (1100–1135) began strengthening Carlisle Castle in stone and enclosing the city with masonry walls. He probably started work on the castle's oldest surviving structure, the great keep, in about 1122, but it was his successors who actually completed the massive stone rectangle. In its heyday, the keep stood over 65 feet (20 metres) high. During the 18th-century Jacobite Rising — an abortive attempt to place the Catholic Bonnie Prince Charlie on the British throne — a first-floor chamber served as a prison. Jacobite prisoners licked the stones of their cells, which were reputedly a source of moisture, to quench their thirst.

### An Imprisoned Queen

Besides the great keep, the inner gatehouse (known as the Captain's Tower), remnants of the royal apartments and other domestic buildings survive from the medieval period. Queen Mary's Tower, named for its most famous prisoner,

Mary, Queen of Scots (1542–87), dates to the 14th century. Partially demolished in 1835, much to the consternation of local citizens who took pride in its associations with the ill-fated monarch, the tower now holds the museum of the King's Own Royal Border Regiment.

During the 1540s, Henry VIII initiated the first of several major modernization projects to refit the castle for artillery. Over the course of the next 350 years, the ongoing presence of the army and the castle's use as a military depot and armoury forced further alterations to the structure, as weapons technology evolved and the fortifications decayed.

From its origins as a substantial ringwork fortification to its most recent role as a military museum, Carlisle Castle has dutifully served its country for over 900 years. Today, the castle no longer fears the impact of battle and ageing on its battlements. The sturdy red walls, which so boldly contrast with the greenery at their base, stand as an everlasting reminder of the turmoil that plagued the borderland between England and Scotland. The castle is managed by English Heritage and is open for visitors throughout the year.

ABOVE: *Just opposite a stone bridge, embedded in the castle ditch, the outer gateway offers access into the outer bailey, which is rimmed by modern barracks buildings. Beyond, the great keep remains Carlisle Castle's strong point.*

## HISTORY

AD 547 – Anglo-Saxon King Ida, the Flamebearer, conquers Northumberland and establishes seat at 'Bebbanburgh'.

7th–8th century AD – The Venerable Bede's History of Northumbria records Bamburgh as a site of major importance.

993 – Vikings destroy the Anglo-Saxon fortress.

1069 – Walcher, Bishop of Durham, gains earldom of Northumberland.

1086 – Robert de Mowbray acquires Bamburgh.

1095 – William II defeats de Mowbray; castle becomes sheriff's administrative centre.

1130s – Eustace Fitzjohn begins stone castle.

1138 – King Stephen grants castle to Henry, Earl of Huntingdon.

1160s – Bamburgh serves as royal stronghold.

1296 – Edward I meets with Scots King John Balliol at castle.

1307 – Isabel de Vescy acquires castle.

1328–33 – Bamburgh withstands sieges by Scots.

1380s – Richard II makes repairs.

1461 – Richard Neville, Earl of Warwick, defeats Lancastrian garrison; after a second siege, Queen Margaret flees but Henry VI stays for nine months.

1464 – Warwick devastates castle with artillery.

1610 – James I of England sells castle to Claudius Forster, Warden of the Middle March.

1704 – Nathaniel Crewe, Bishop of Durham, begins restoring great keep.

1758 – Dr John Sharpe, Archdeacon of Northumberland, adds school, library and coastguard station.

1894 – 1st Lord Armstrong demolishes portions of original castle during remodelling project.

1940s – Castle becomes military headquarters during Second World War.

1971 – Discovery of Anglo-Saxon coins, a sword and the 'Bamburgh Beast'.

1996 – Bamburgh Research Project founded.

1998–2002 – Excavation of Bowl Hole.

# Bamburgh Castle

Dominating a craggy ridge about 150 feet (46 metres) above the Northumbrian shoreline, majestic Bamburgh Castle has capably served kings and commoners for almost a millennium. Views across the tidal sands separating the mainland from Holy Island emphasize Bamburgh's strategic importance to the Normans and also to their predecessors, the Anglo-Saxons, who transformed Northumbria into a cultural and religious centre well before the invasion of 1066. Having Iron Age and Roman roots, and legendary associations with the Arthurian knights Sir Lancelot and Sir Galahad, Bamburgh's heritage extends back at least to the 1st century BC. In the guise of its present owners, the Armstrongs, the fortress continues to flourish 21 centuries later.

### A Great Tower

Commanded by a powerful great tower and enclosed by a masonry wall that traces the perimeter of the crag upon which it stands, Bamburgh is a classic example of a stone-enclosure castle. The layout of the medieval castle, its three baileys and rectangular keep survive. Structurally, the four-storey, turreted tower represents a typical Norman rectangular keep, and it is more than likely that it dates to the 12th century. However, historians differ on who actually built the self-sufficient castle-within-a-castle. Some reasonably believe Henry I or Henry II (1154–89) erected the great tower. Others suggest David I of Scotland (1124–53) or his son, Henry, Earl of Huntingdon, may have spearheaded the project. Whoever actually built the imposing tower, it remains the medieval castle's most impressive – and lasting – feature.

### Archaeological Gems

Since the late 1960s, archaeologists have routinely excavated the grounds and surrounding landscape. Discoveries have been numerous. Within the west bailey, potsherds (pottery shards) and traces of foodstuffs, including fish bones and cereal grains, have been discovered which date back to the Iron Age and the Roman era. Evidence has also

ABOVE: *Bamburgh Castle's impressive armoury features items dating as far back as the 15th century, as well as muskets and pikes readied for use during the Napoleonic Wars.*

ABOVE LEFT: *Cannons face the North Sea from their strategic positions along the battlements, poised to defend the castle from waterborne invasion.*

been found of a post-Roman beacon that was used to warn of raids from the sea. Then, in 1971, the late Dr Brian Hope-Taylor found the tiny 'Bamburgh Beast', which is arguably the most enchanting archaeological find from the castle. Reminiscent of the artwork that adorns the famous Lindisfarne Gospels, the small, hand-crafted gold plaque features a stylized creature and clearly ties the site to the Anglo-Saxons.

In recent years, the Bamburgh Research Project has employed standard excavation practices, used ground-penetrating radar and conducted geophysical surveys to locate the long-hidden remains of medieval structures, medieval glass, bone implements and other artefacts. They have also pinpointed the site of an Anglo-Saxon burial ground, known as Bowl Hole, which dates to as early as the 7th century.

## 'Probably the Finest'

Bamburgh Castle truly is one of England's grandest and most historic monuments. Its riches not only include the great keep and grand interiors, but also a vast archaeological heritage, much of which still awaits discovery. The Armstrong family opens their home, 'probably the finest castle in England', during the spring and summer months for an entrance fee.

BELOW: *The basalt outcrop supporting mighty Bamburgh Castle has experienced centuries of human activity. Long before the Normans settled the stronghold in the 11th century and began constructing the superb enclosure castle, prehistoric peoples, Romans, Anglo-Saxons and Vikings landed at its rugged base.*

## HISTORY

11th century – Gilbert Tyson (de Tesson), William the Conqueror's standard-bearer, acquires property at Alnwick.

1096 – Yvo de Vescy begins castle.

1138 – Eustace Fitzjohn, Baron of Alnwick, surrenders castle to David I of Scotland.

1172 & 1174 – William the Lion unsuccessfully besieges castle.

1184 – Castle passes to Eustace de Vescy, William the Lion's son-in-law.

1213 – King John orders castle's demolition in retaliation for de Vescy's role in barons' rebellion.

1215 – De Vescy joins Scots King Alexander to invade Northumberland; King John burns Alnwick Castle.

1297 – Scottish rebel William Wallace unsuccessfully attacks castle; Bishop of Durham acquires castle upon the death of the last de Vescy heir.

1309 – Henry, 1st Lord Percy of Alnwick, purchases castle from Bishop Anthony Bek; initiates major reconstruction programme.

1424 & 1448 – Scots besiege and burn castle.

1460s & 1470s – Possession alternates between Yorkists and Lancastrians during War of the Roses.

1462 – Scottish army, led by Queen Margaret, seizes castle.

1489 – 'The Mob' murders Henry, 4th Earl, for imposing an unpopular tax.

1568 – Thomas Percy, 7th Earl, surrenders castle to Sir John Forster, Warden of the Middle Marches, and is executed in 1572.

1584 – Imprisoned in Tower of London for plotting with Mary, Queen of Scots, Henry, 8th Earl, dies under mysterious circumstances.

1632 – 9th Earl is imprisoned as he is suspected of a role in the Gunpowder Plot; Percy family leaves Northumberland.

1755 – Sir Hugh Smithson (later Percy), 12th Earl, having married a female heir to the estate, employs architect Robert Adam to recreate castle interiors.

Late 19th century – Restoration work begins on castle.

# Alnwick Castle

William Shakespeare (1564–1616) chronicled the history of one of England's most powerful medieval families, the Percys, in his plays *Richard II* and *Henry IV*. The Percy legacy, Alnwick Castle, remains a remarkable tribute to the impact of the Earls and Dukes of Northumberland on British history and to the skills of the architects who designed the fortress. The Northumberlands have continuously occupied the grand residence near the Scottish border for well over 700 years. England's second largest inhabited castle after Windsor (see pages 43–5), Alnwick has endured a tumultuous history filled with actions that pitted the Northumberlands against the English monarchy and also against the Scots.

## Lord and Rebel

Arguably the best known and most controversial of the lords of Northumberland, Henry, 4th Lord Percy and 1st Earl of Northumberland (1342–1409), actively participated in England's wars against the Scots and also fought with his king in France. However, in 1399, Richard II's (1377–99) accusations of treason against the Percys provoked a rebellion and the accession of the Percys' favourite, Henry IV (1399–1413), to the English throne.

Four years later, the Percys led another rebellion, this time against the allegedly ungrateful king they had placed on the throne. Even after royalists seized Percy and killed his son, Henry 'Hotspur' Percy (1364–1403), at the Battle of Shrewsbury, Percy supporters held on to Alnwick Castle. They capitulated only when confronted by the king's mighty siege engines.

Freed the following year, Lord Percy joined Archbishop Richard Scrope's (c. 1350–1405) rebellion against Henry IV in 1405. After royalist troops defeated the garrison at Alnwick, Percy fled to Scotland. In 1408, he tried one last time to overthrow the king, but was killed by the Sheriff of Yorkshire at Bramham Moor.

In the midst of this turmoil, the 1st Earl of Northumberland began Alnwick Castle's transformation into the splendid ducal residence occupied by his descendants to this day. Highlighted by lush green grasses and enclosed by a sturdy towered curtain wall, Percy's work, which includes the Middle Gateway, the well-preserved Constable's Tower and a watchtower named Hotspur's Seat, enwraps the middle bailey. Erected in about 1350, the 1st Earl's most impressive addition, the great keep, dominates the site.

**OPPOSITE ABOVE:** *An intricately carved Greek soldier raises his shield as if ready for battle.*

**OPPOSITE:** *Crowned with life-sized stone sentinels, Henry Percy's twin octagonal towers project the sheer power of Alnwick's majestic great keep.*

**BELOW:** *Steadfastly guarding the grounds of Alnwick Castle, the Percy heraldic lion graces the battlemented walls enclosing the outer bailey, fearlessly reminding passers-by of the impact the Dukes of Northumberland had on English history.*

## Rebirth and Restoration

Although heavily refurbished during the 18th and 19th centuries, Alnwick Castle retains its original medieval plan, which consisted of a low mound (possibly a Norman motte), a circular keep, two baileys and a multi-towered, irregular curtain wall. In 1755, Hugh, the 1st Duke of Northumberland (1715–86), hired the incomparable architect, Robert Adam (1728–92), to recreate his ancestral castle. However, almost a century later, the 4th Duke turned to Anthony Salvin (1799–1881) to complete the castle's rebirth. Salvin pulled down most of Adam's modifications, and restored the residence to its medieval grandeur.

Fronted by Percy's octagonal towers and encompassed by a seven-towered wall, the four-storey, polygonal keep commands a place of pride on top of the grass-laden medieval mound. Patrolling the battlements, life-sized stone soldiers stalwartly guard the grounds below. Visible from quite a distance, the skilfully carved sentinels would have presented a roaming enemy

with the impression that a formidable garrison of soldiers awaited their approach. Attackers knew their best decision was to retreat with their lives intact. Even today, the stone men exude a quiet but steadfast presence, and rank high among Alnwick's most alluring treasures.

In recent years, the fictional wizard Harry Potter practised his powers at Hogwarts' School of Witchcraft and Wizardry, which was portrayed by the illustrious castle in the film versions of J.K. Rowling's magical tales.

Ralph George Algernon Percy, 12th Duke of Northumberland, continues the proud tradition established by his ancestors so long ago. No longer fearing attack, Alnwick Castle has successfully made the transformation from a rudimentary earth-and-timber fortress to a palatial residence, and rightfully proclaims itself as one of England's finest stately homes. The noble structure instils awe in the beholder, as it undoubtedly did in Henry Percy's day. The castle is open daily to visitors for an entrance fee between April and October.

# Warkworth Castle

Prized by kings on both sides of the border for its strategic position in northern England, Warkworth Castle radiates the energy of its turbulent past. The scene of bloody battles, family rivalries and alternating alliances, the entrancing ruins testify to the rigorous persistence of the British nobility despite assault on all fronts. Over time, the Northumbrian stronghold emerged from a simple motte-and-bailey castle into one of the most formidable stone fortresses of its day. Now largely a ruin, Warkworth Castle documents the entirety of England's castle-building history. And, it possesses a feature found nowhere else in the realm – a magnificent cross-like keep.

### Wardens of the Scottish Marches

Lords of Warkworth from the 14th century, the Percys, who ruled over Northumberland, were tasked to quell the rebellious Scots. The family took their role as Wardens of the Scottish Marches (borders) seriously and buttressed the castle against further attacks from the north. Yet, for the Percys, owning Warkworth Castle meant much more: they had expanded their power

ABOVE: *The best-preserved face of the great keep dominates the inner bailey at Warkworth Castle, from where guests, and the lords themselves, could admire the unique building.*

BELOW: *Fronted with a substantial gatehouse and the polygonal Carrickfergus Tower to the west and the square Montagu Tower to the east, the enormous outer bailey contained all the buildings the Percys could require – including an entire church!*

## HISTORY

AD 737 – Ceolwulf, King of Northumbria, gives Warkworth lands to the monks of Lindisfarne.

11th century – Osbert, last Northumbrian king, retakes estates.

1158 – Henry II grants 'Werceworde' to Roger FitzRichard, who later receives honour of Clavering in Essex.

1174 – William the Lion besieges castle and slaughters local citizens in the church.

1199 – Robert FitzRoger instigates major building project at the site.

1327 – Scottish king, Robert the Bruce, besieges castle.

1328 – Scots and English sign peace treaty; Claverings retain castle.

1332 – Edward III grants castle to Henry, 2nd Lord Percy of Alnwick.

1377 – Henry, 4th Lord Percy, becomes 1st Earl of Northumberland.

1403 – Percy and his son, 'Hotspur', use castle to plot against Henry IV.

1405 – Archbishop Scrope fails to place Percy on English throne; Percy flees to Scotland; Henry IV uses cannons to force castle's surrender; Warkworth passes to king's son, John.

1416 – Henry V restores castle to Henry Percy, 2nd Earl.

1462 – Richard Neville, Earl of Warwick, stages assaults on Bamburgh and Alnwick from Warkworth; John Neville, Lord Montagu, acquires castle.

1471 – Henry Percy, 4th Earl of Northumberland, regains possession.

1572 – Scots sell Thomas Percy, 7th Earl, to Elizabeth I, who orders his beheading.

1574 – Henry Percy, 8th Earl, regains castle.

1605 – Sir Ralph Grey allows castle to decay.

1648 – Castle occupied by parliamentarian forces during English Civil War.

1672 – John Clarke, estate auditor, quarries castle for building material.

1922 – Castle placed into State care.

ABOVE: *Planted atop the original earthen motte, Warkworth's formidable keep still watches over the River Coquet and displays its builder's ingenuity and social status to all passers-by.*

base within the kingdom, controlled three of the kingdom's sturdiest and most impressive fortresses – Warkworth, Alnwick (see pages 22–4) and Bamburgh (see pages 20–21) – and ruled northern England like kings. Their future lay as king-makers, rebellious conspirators and powerful castle-builders.

## A Unique Keep

Late in the 14th century, Henry, 4th Lord Percy, added Warkworth Castle's defining feature – the unique cross-like keep – to the northernmost corner of the gated stone enclosure. From above, the unique structure resembles a cross that has been superimposed on a square. Riddled with passageways leading to spiral staircases and a myriad of chambers, including the great hall, kitchen block, solar (private chambers of the lord of the castle), bedchambers, the chapel, chancel and sacristy, the keep rose for three storeys. The maze-like building also accommodated beer and wine cellars. Adorned throughout with the Percy lion, the great tower vividly dramatized the family's status.

The stately Lion Tower in the inner bailey also expresses the self-importance of the Percys. Originally serving as the porch into the hall and the neighbouring church, the structure was later used as accommodation. Today, the ungainly building stands on its own, seemingly out of place. Yet, the skilfully sculpted lion forever roars a silent tribute to the Earls of Northumberland and their descendants.

## The Castle Church

While most castles contained a chapel for regular worship, few held a collegiate church within their walls. Yet, Warkworth was an exception to the rule in more ways than one. By building an entire church in the centre of the inner bailey, the Percys undoubtedly intended to symbolically reconfirm their supreme importance to England. Now represented by its cruciform foundations, the collegiate church once housed a group of priests who sang mass and prayed for their benefactor.

During the 19th century, Algernon, 4th Duke of Northumberland (1792–1865), rescued Warkworth Castle from complete decay. Employing the famed architect, Anthony Salvin, the Duke consolidated the ruins and partially renovated the keep to make it habitable. Today, the site remains a splendid tribute to the ambitions of one of England's most distinguished and long-lived families. Warkworth Castle is maintained by English Heritage and is open to the public throughout the year for an entrance fee.

# Kenilworth Castle

Lauded in the 17th century by the antiquarian Sir William Dugdale (1605–86) as 'the glory of these parts', Kenilworth Castle in Warwickshire has set the scene for drama, novels and films throughout its history. At one time enwrapped by a 100-acre (40.5-hectare) artificial lake and decorated with lavish Tudor gardens, this formidable fortress capably withstood a protracted siege and also served as a luxurious residence primed to impress even the most fastidious of royal individuals. Today, the building's red sandstone masonry boldly contrasts with the verdant landscape that surrounds it, and the ruins pay unflinching tribute to the castle's celebrated owners and honoured guests.

## The Great Mere

While deep, water-filled moats adequately defended many medieval castles, the waters of two tiny streams provided a daunting barrier to enemy assaults on Kenilworth Castle. The combined strength of the stone structures and water defences, the first of their kind in the realm, made the castle virtually invulnerable to a siege. Only the complex water defences and concentric design of Caerphilly Castle (see pages 110–13) rivalled Kenilworth.

BELOW: *Originally adorning the porchway to John of Gaunt's Hall, the stunning doorway into Leicester's Gatehouse displays the grandeur that once bedecked much of Kenilworth Castle.*

ABOVE: *The ruined shell of Leicester's building. Built by Robert Dudley in the late 16th century, each of the three storeys contained luxury accommodation and afforded grand vistas of the Great Mere.*

## HISTORY

Early 12th century – Geoffrey de Clinton, Henry I's chamberlain and treasurer, begins castle at Kenilworth.

Early to mid-13th century – Damming of the Finham and Inchford streams creates the Great Mere.

1264 – Simon de Montfort the elder imprisons Henry III's brother, Richard, Earl of Cornwall, and his son, Edmund, at the castle.

1265 – Simon de Montfort the younger escapes death by swimming across the Great Mere to the castle.

1326 – Edward II signs his abdication papers while imprisoned at castle.

1359 – Edward III's son, John of Gaunt, acquires Kenilworth and Duchy of Lancaster; spends great sums to convert the castle into a pleasure palace.

1553 – Edward VI grants the castle-cum-palace to John Dudley, Duke of Northumberland; Mary Tudor executes Dudley for his role in placing Lady Jane Grey on the English throne and the castle reverts to the Crown.

1563 – Elizabeth I bestows castle on her favourite courtier, Robert Dudley, Earl of Leicester and John Dudley's son.

1649 – During the English Civil War, parliamentarian troops slight the decaying fortress and drain its water defences.

1937 – Sir John Davenport Siddely, Lord Kenilworth, buys the ruin of the castle and turns it over to the State.

ABOVE: *The undulating grounds beneath Kenilworth's great red keep come alive when modern knights prepare for battle, as they did in the 13th century during Simon de Montfort's rebellion against Henry III.*

During the Barons' Rebellion in 1266, Henry III (1216–72) tested Kenilworth's water defences, known as the Great Mere, against a defiant garrison loyal to Simon de Montfort, 6th Earl of Leicester (*c.* 1208–65), and his son, also named Simon. The immense waters forced the attackers to construct their siege engines well away from their target. Even though the king's men hammered the rebel fortress for over nine months, the extra distance severely restricted their ability to pull down the heavy masonry structures. At times their stones crashed in mid-air into missiles fired from inside the castle. Royalist troops also attempted a lake crossing using a fleet of ships from Chester, but their effort failed miserably. De Montfort's men eventually surrendered – but only when their food supplies had run out and disease had taken its toll.

Besides more than capably fulfilling its military role, Kenilworth Castle often acted as an entertainment venue. In 1279, Roger de Mortimer (*c.* 1231–82) held a raucous medieval tournament at the castle, treating the water defences as the star attraction and making special use of the tiltyard. While their ladies watched, 100 knights competed for three days in the traditional joust and in a new game called 'the Round Table'.

## Elizabeth and Leicester

Three centuries later, Robert Dudley, Earl of Leicester, (*c.* 1532–88) dramatized his passion for Elizabeth I with one of the most widely acclaimed events of his day. For 19 days in 1575, Elizabeth's favourite wined, dined and fêted his queen and her entourage of 31 barons, numerous ladies-in-waiting and 400 servants. Housing Elizabeth in Leicester's Building, Dudley ensured she had the most stylish accommodation. Using the Great Mere as the backdrop for the festivities, Dudley organized a wondrous water pageant, masques, fireworks, hunting and bear baiting, music, dancing, minstrel shows, mystery plays and, of course, feasting. In all, Dudley spent an estimated £100,000, bankrupting himself for his queen's amusement.

Even in ruin, Kenilworth Castle's vivid rust-coloured walls still cause hearts to flutter, as Elizabeth's must have when Dudley entertained her so many centuries ago. Presently managed by English Heritage, the castle is open to the public throughout the year for a fee.

**RIGHT:** *A series of massive Norman arches supported the upper levels of Kenilworth Castle's great keep. Now little more than a shell, the powerful, self-sufficient structure was built to stand alone during a siege. Its most formidable foe, Cromwell's parliamentarian troops, pulled down the northern wall and rendered the stronghold useless for future military action.*

**BELOW:** *The expansive grounds enclosing Kenilworth Castle once flowed with water. The Great Mere not only created a formidable barrier to assaults during the siege of 1266, it also served as the venue for Robert Dudley's extravagant water pageant, which honoured Queen Elizabeth I's 19-day visit in 1575.*

# HISTORY

AD 914 – Ethelfleda, the daughter of Alfred the Great, fortifies Saxon settlement at Warwick.

1088 – Henry de Beaumont (or de Newburgh) becomes constable and 1st Earl of Warwick.

1260s – Shell keep and stone curtain wall added.

1263 – William Mauduit becomes Earl of Warwick by right of marriage to Margaret de Newburgh.

1264 – John Giffard, constable at Kenilworth Castle, holds Earl of Warwick and his wife for ransom during Barons' Rebellion.

1312 – Guy de Beauchamp, 10th Earl of Warwick, imprisons Piers Gaveston, the favourite of Edward II at castle; Gaveston's execution takes place on nearby Blacklow Hill.

1329 – Thomas de Beauchamp, 11th Earl of Warwick, extends castle defences.

1431 – Richard de Beauchamp, 13th Earl of Warwick, supervises Joan of Arc's execution in France.

1450 – Richard Neville, the 'Kingmaker', becomes Earl of Warwick.

1469 – Neville imprisons Edward IV at Warwick Castle.

1471 – Edward IV grants castle to his brother, George Plantagenet, Duke of Clarence.

1483 – Richard III begins great keep, but only completes Bear and Clarence Towers.

1547 – Edward VI grants castle and earldom to John Dudley.

1618 – James I grants title of Earl of Warwick – but not the castle – to Robert, Lord Rich.

1621 – Sir Fulke Greville becomes 1st Lord Brooke.

1642 – 2nd Lord Brooke garrisons castle for Parliament and thwarts Royalist attack.

1695 – William III visits castle.

1759 – Francis Greville regains earldom.

Late 18th century – Refurbishment of State Rooms; Lancelot 'Capability' Brown landscapes grounds.

1978 – Tussauds Group purchase castle from 37th Earl and initiate ongoing restoration programme.

# Warwick Castle

Touted by the Tussauds Group as 'Britain's Greatest Medieval Experience', Warwick Castle has become something akin to a theme park. Special events, medieval banquets and a suite of rooms enlivened with wax figures of the Earl and Countess of Warwick preparing for a royal party create an almost circus-like atmosphere. Yet, underneath the glitter and fanfare lies the real attraction – the great medieval castle itself. Displaying the stately splendour that showcased the status and ambitions of the Earls of Warwick for 800 years, Warwick Castle represents the best of castle-building in England.

### A Formidable Stronghold

Peacocks perched in the trees crow their welcome as visitors make their way out of the car park towards the castle's main entrance. The effect is almost surreal, and pulls one's attention away from the present in anticipation of a journey back to the Middle Ages. The powerful curtain wall points ahead to the twin-towered barbican and gatehouse, which, when traversed, opens not only to the magnificent inner courtyard, but also magically transports the senses back in time. Surrounded on three sides by a dry ditch and the River Avon on the fourth, this powerful structure is a classic stone-enclosure castle.

### Untested Defences

Begun as an earth-and-timber fortress shortly after the Norman Conquest, Warwick Castle displays relics from every castle-building era. Today, the well-preserved motte and its ruined shell keep sit discreetly at the western end of the stone fortress. Commanded at strategic points by lofty polygonal towers that are linked together by a wall-walk, this formidable stronghold would have capably withstood even those most intensive of sieges, had it had the opportunity. Only weakly attacked on two occasions, these massive defences never faced an onslaught. As its lord supported Parliament against Charles I (1625–49) in the English Civil War, Warwick even managed to avoid the slighting that ruined so many other castles in the 17th century.

### Warwick's Great Towers

Two towers rise either side of the great gatehouse – the incomparable quatrefoil Caesar's Tower and the 12-sided Guy's Tower. Standing over 120 feet (36.5 metres) high, these 14th-century towers offer unobstructed views over the lush Warwickshire countryside, contain a maze of rooms and fine staircases and give access to the intact wall-walk. Still accessible via a steep staircase, the dreary dungeon sits at the base of the Caesar's Tower. Besides the medieval torture devices, the chamber's most haunting feature is the oubliette, a tiny, windowless chamber in which prisoners were kept in total darkness, with barely enough room to lie down. Food and water were delivered via a trap-door in the ceiling.

**ABOVE:** *Stained-glass windows grace the stone walls throughout the State Apartments. This yellow composite neo-classical design welcomes visitors to the great hall.*

**OPPOSITE:** *Strategically placed to guard vital communications routes through the English countryside, castles such as majestic Warwick – shown here overlooking the crumbling bridge across the River Avon – displayed the power, status and wealth of the kingdom's nobility, including the Neville Earls of Warwick, known to history as 'Kingmakers'.*

**ABOVE:** *The battlemented curtain wall sweeps over the original Norman motte, built upon William the Conqueror's orders in 1068.*

**BELOW:** *An iron-spiked portcullis and rows of rectangular murder holes in the ceiling beyond are ready to challenge any attack on the gatehouse.*

Across the courtyard stands the 14th-century Watergate Tower. This is also known as the Ghost Tower, as the spectre of the murdered Elizabethan and Jacobean politician and poet Sir Fulke Greville (1554–1628), who owned the castle from 1604, is said to haunt it. The squat tower provided access to the River Avon, which flows at its base and functioned as a natural moat. Across the river, half-timbered and brick houses line the closest lanes. Historically associated with the castle as quarters for servants and other workers, these well-maintained medieval homes offer a fascinating glimpse into the less glamorous, more mundane aspects of castle life. To reach the castle, employees originally crossed a stone bridge, the ruins of which still defiantly withstand the waters of the Avon. Visitors are welcome to explore the exterior of these houses, but should respect the privacy of their owners.

**Life Inside**

Back inside Warwick Castle, the State Apartments express the grandeur of an earl's life, much as it was during the 18th and 19th centuries. Visitors can explore the Great Hall, the State Dining Room, the Red, Green and Cedar drawing rooms, the Queen Anne Bedroom, the Blue Boudoir and the Chapel. Decorated with gilded plasterwork ceilings, shining armour, skilfully carved woodwork and sumptuous furniture, these graceful rooms contrast colourfully with the castle's intimidating grey walls.

Warwick Castle contains a treasure trove of fascinating memorabilia. A magnificent medieval stronghold, it honours the memory of the powerful Earls of Warwick, who made kings and removed their enemies. The building is open to visitors throughout the year for an entrance fee.

# Goodrich Castle

Admired by the Romantic poet William Wordsworth (1770–1850) as 'the noblest ruin in Herefordshire', Goodrich Castle crowns a craggy outcrop above the River Wye, just south-west of Ross-on-Wye. Guarding the river crossing between England and Wales, the heavily fortified complex of military buildings boldly demonstrated the power of the Norman Marcher lords in the borderlands. With its tremendous towers and an intimidating ditch formed from a natural chasm in the bedrock, the quadrangular stronghold retains an air of invincibility. Rising directly from its red sandstone base, the well-preserved walls are perhaps only slightly less capable of withstanding a siege, as they did during the English Civil War.

## A Monumental Building Programme

Probably named for the Anglo-Saxon thegn (or thane, a low-ranking noble), Godric de Mappestone, who held neighbouring Hulle (Howle) in 1086, an earth-and-timber fortress first dominated the site. Almost a century later, Henry II fortified Godric's castle against the Welsh, replacing the primitive

BELOW: *The light grey sandstone masonry defining the great keep contrasts clearly with the darker stonework used for the two powerful corner towers.*

ABOVE: *The original arched first-floor entrance into the great keep later served as a decorative window, which featured trefoiled lights and carved columns.*

## HISTORY

1101 – First mention of castle at the site.

1160s – Construction begins on great keep.

1204 – King John grants castle and surrounding lands to William Marshal, Earl of Pembroke, who begins transformation to stone.

Early 13th century – Towered curtain wall added (only chapel and foundations at base of south-west tower survive).

1247 – William de Valence becomes Earl of Pembroke.

1260s and 1280s – Major building programmes extend castle; corner towers, gatehouse and other stone buildings erected.

1324 – Elizabeth Comyn inherits castle upon the death of her uncle, Aymer de Valence, but is imprisoned there by Hugh le Despenser.

1326 – Richard, 2nd Baron Talbot, Elizabeth's husband, seizes the castle.

1381 – Castle refortified in anticipation of attack from rival Marcher lords.

1442 – Talbots become Earls of Shrewsbury.

Late 15th century – John, 3rd Earl of Shrewsbury, relinquishes castle to Edward IV, who turns control over to William Herbert.

1616 – Upon the death of Gilbert Talbot, the 7th Earl, Goodrich Castle passes by right of marriage to Elizabeth Talbot's husband, Henry Grey, Earl of Kent.

Early 17th century – Castle kitchen acquires running water.

1740 – Admiral Thomas Griffin buys Goodrich and begins its restoration.

1920 – Owner Mrs. Edmund Bosanquet places castle into State care.

1920s – Commissioners of Works begin consolidation of ruin.

point. Built to confuse and confine an enemy, the D-shaped outwork forced attackers to turn twice before they could cross the ditch and clamber up the steep ramp to assault the gatehouse.

## Roundheads and Cavaliers

During the English Civil War, mighty Goodrich Castle stood its ground. Although garrisoned with 100 parliamentary troops in 1643, control of the castle passed to Sir Henry Lingen, a staunch supporter of Charles I, in 1645. Early the following year, Colonel John Birch and his parliamentarian forces made a sudden assault on the castle. Bolstered by the power of Roaring Meg, a specially cast bombard (cannon) that was capable of hurtling a shot of over 200lbs (90kg), the besiegers pummelled the walls relentlessly. Sappers undermined the north-west tower. Royalist guards died and the castle's stables burned. Having only four barrels of gunpowder and aware that the parliamentarians itched to finish off the defences, Lingen's men finally waved the white flag and surrendered. Tradition has it that they strode out of Goodrich Castle to a tune, long since lost, called 'Sir Henry Lingen's Fancy'. Birch accepted their dignified surrender and allowed the royalists to keep their lives.

Goodrich Castle was slighted in 1647 and fell into ruin. The Countess of Kent, who now owned the castle, received £1,000 against the damages, but chose not to rebuild.

## Lost Splendour

Besides having ponderous defences, the castle functioned as a fine residence. It supported a chapel tower, the great hall and kitchen range on the west and south sides and private apartments immediately to the north. Today, the blocky ruins belie the buildings' medieval splendour.

English Heritage maintains Goodrich Castle, which is open daily throughout the year for an entrance fee. Springing suddenly into view, the hulking red ruins still startle the senses as they did when Wordsworth explored the site in the late 18th century.

ABOVE: *Traditionally known as Macbeth's or Macmac's Tower, the great 12th-century keep dominates the inner bailey. Immediately alongside the present ground floor entrance, a gap in the masonry leads into the windowless dungeon.*

OPPOSITE: *Rising from the depths of the ditch almost to the battlements, the pyramidal spurred buttresses on the south-eastern corner tower merged masonry with bedrock to form an impregnable barrier to enemy undermining.*

stronghold with an ungainly grey keep, which is the site's oldest surviving structure.

Conveyed in 1247 by right of marriage from the Marshal Earls of Pembroke to William de Valence (c. 1226–96), Henry III's half-brother, Goodrich Castle became the focus of a monumental building programme. Adopting the pretentious building style used by his nephew, Edward I (1272–1307), in North Wales, de Valence bolstered the castle with three mammoth drum towers, a round-fronted gatehouse and thick curtain walls. He also added a walled courtyard next to the keep and built several ancillary structures, including a chapel.

After William de Valence's death, his widow, Joan, continued his work at the castle, which then passed to their son, Aymer, in 1307. Aymer's greatest contribution was the helmet-like barbican, which protected the main access

**ABOVE:** *One of the White Tower's most enchanting features is the Chapel of St John the Evangelist, which retains its medieval atmosphere. Now plain, the walls once boasted brightly painted decorations. The chapel displays fine examples of Norman architecture.*

wall. Henry also established a royal menagerie inside the castle, which housed an elephant, bears, lions and other exotic animals that were presented to him by the crown heads of several European nations.

Later in the 13th century, Edward I transformed the Tower of London into a fine concentric fortress comparable to those that he built in North Wales (see pages 124–35). Spending over £21,000, this great castle-building king filled in the moat and enclosed the fortress with yet another, albeit lower, towered curtain wall that was fitted with heavily defended twin-towered gatehouses. He also added St Thomas's Tower, a luxurious range equipped with a water-gate for access to and from the Thames. Now known as Traitor's Gate, this port acquired its ominous appellation after the prisoners who

passed through the gated archway on their way to confinement and the execution block. Among these were three of the most famous victims of Henry VIII: Sir Thomas More (1478–1535), whose name adorns the building, Anne Boleyn (*c.* 1507–36) and Catherine Howard (*c.* 1521–42).

Besides its role as a powerful fortress, a prison and the monarch's zoo, the Tower of London acquired other responsibilities over time. Edward I built a royal mint inside the castle and added a treasury to house the Crown Jewels. Now displayed in the Jewel House, the Crown Jewels remain one of the castle's glories. The Tudors expanded the Tower of London's role as a prison and staged scores of political executions on Tower Green and on Tower Hill, where a plaque commemorates the 125 prisoners who lost their lives there.

LEFT: *Constructed by Edward I in the late 13th century, the twin-towered Byward Tower offers access into the outer bailey (or ward) of the Tower of London. The innermost of three gatehouses, the Byward Tower probably acquired its curious name from its position 'by the ward'.*

By the late 17th century, the castle's role as a state prison diminished. The Office of Ordnance began to occupy the site and with them came munitions stores, military workshops, a barracks for the permanent garrison and gun batteries. The fortress also contained two armouries. In the 1840s, the Army constructed the North Bastion, Waterloo Barracks and other structures in response to the Chartist Movement, which demonstrated against the social and political ills of the day, and the mint, zoo and records office were transferred elsewhere in London. Beginning in the 1850s, Queen Victoria (1837–1901) and Prince Albert (1819–61) recognized the Tower's importance as a national monument and began restoring the castle's medieval appearance.

## A National Symbol

Today, London's mighty castle remains garrisoned by the military, the most visible of whom are the knowledgeable Yeoman Warders, popularly known as 'Beefeaters'. They have safeguarded the castle since early in its history and now regale visitors with stories of treason, beheadings, torture and ghostly apparitions. Like the ever-present ravens, the Beefeaters are living symbols of national pride and perseverance and are emblematic of England's most historic castle – the Tower of London.

Managed by Historic Royal Palaces, the Tower of London is open daily throughout the year for an entrance fee, and the castle's complexity and history more than compensate any queues. The castle patently deserves its status as a World Heritage Site, achieved in 1988.

ABOVE: *In recent years, officials at the castle determined that the ageing portcullis, seen here behind the windlass, the engine that raised and lowered the powerful gate, still has the ability to bar unwanted access. Positioned over the gate passage in the Byward Tower, it is the castle's only operational portcullis.*

# Rochester Castle

## HISTORY

1st century AD – Romans extend Watling Street (the road from Dover) to the River Medway.

7th century – Saxons found episcopal see at Rochester.

1088 – William II besieges castle, the head-quarters for rebels led by Bishop Odo of Bayeux, who surrenders; Bishop Gundulf begins stone-enclosure castle.

1127 – Henry I grants custody of castle in perpetuity to see of Canterbury; Archbishop William de Corbeil constructs great keep.

1215 – King John seizes castle, then held by Archbishop Stephen Langton.

1220 – Henry III builds round tower on keep and smaller round tower on curtain wall.

1264 – Rebel barons Simon de Montfort and Gilbert de Clare besiege castle, but retreat 10 days later.

1314 – Queen Isabel of Scotland, Robert the Bruce's wife, is imprisoned in castle.

1367–70 – Edward III completes major rebuilding programme.

1378 – Richard II begins northern bastion.

1381 – Peasants' Revolt damages castle.

1416 – Sigismund, Emperor of Germany, arrives with 1,000 knights.

1540 – Henry VIII meets Anne of Cleves, later his fourth wife.

1610 – James I sells castle to Sir Anthony Weldon.

1780 – Proposals to demolish castle are rejected.

1870 – Earl of Jersey transforms grounds into gardens.

1884 – City of Rochester buys castle.

1965 – State acquires castle.

1984 – English Heritage takes over care of castle.

Ideally poised to guard the medieval bridge that spanned the River Medway, Rochester Castle in Kent dominates the urban landscape it inhabits just south-east of London. Once known as Durobrivae, 'the stronghold by the bridge', the Roman town provided ready-made defensive walls for the Normans who settled there a thousand years later. The 19th-century novelist, Charles Dickens (1812–70), who lived in Rochester and wandered its ancient lanes, lauded the castle's majestic ruins in *The Pickwick Papers* (1837) and *The Mystery of Edwin Drood* (1870).

### Dickensian Epithets

*'What a sight for an antiquarian!' were the very words which fell from Mr. Pickwick's mouth, as he applied his telescope to his eye. 'Ah! fine place,' said the stranger (Mr Augustus Snodgrass), 'glorious pile – frowning walls – tottering arches – dark nooks – crumbling staircases.'*

Today, the Dickensian epithets still apply. The tallest of its type in England, Rochester Castle's classic Norman keep rises 113 feet (34.4 metres) and measures 70 square feet (6.5 square metres). Riddled with stairways, windows, mural chambers and garderobes, the shell of the great keep resembles a maze. Its massive walls vary from 11 to 13 feet (3.4 to 4 metres) in thickness and once enclosed four levels of chambers, the most important of which was the second storey, as it held the great hall and great chamber

and quite possibly served as the Archbishop of Canterbury's state apartments.

## A Medieval Siege

So strong were the walls of Rochester's keep that for two months during the Barons' Rebellion of late 1215 the castle withstood almost constant battering from King John's formidable siege engines. Seizing Rochester Castle in order to prevent the king from returning to London, William d'Albini garrisoned the stronghold with rebel supporters. In response, John swiftly marched to the castle and personally commanded royalist troops in one of England's most noteworthy medieval sieges.

Effectively employing great stone-throwing machines, John's men breached the castle's curtain wall, but the garrison refused to surrender. The king then ordered sappers to undermine the south-eastern angle of the great tower. Propping the mine with timber beams, the men packed the tunnel with 40 fatty pigs and set them alight. The raging fire burned the timber props, causing

the earth to collapse beneath the angular corner, which also crumbled. The rebels retreated to the opposite side of the keep and continued to resist. On the verge of starvation and forced to eat horseflesh, the defenders finally capitulated.

## Rochester Ruined

Despite the best efforts of kings Henry III and Edward III (1327–77) to repair the site, Rochester Castle fell into ruin. During the 19th and 20th centuries, its owners consolidated the grand stronghold by the River Medway, which had narrowly escaped demolition in the 18th century. Together, the Norman-era buildings effectively dramatized the vital link between Church and State during the Middle Ages.

English Heritage now cares for the site, which they open to the public for an entrance fee throughout the year. Rochester Castle remains every bit the 'magnificent ruin' described by Mr Snodgrass in *The Pickwick Papers*, 'with all the poetic fervour that distinguished him, when they came in sight of the fine old castle'.

**ABOVE:** *Originally constructed with four rectangular corner towers, the south-eastern angle of the great keep now sports a cylindrical tower intended to repel more easily stone missiles and thwart undermining.*

**OPPOSITE ABOVE:** *Seen from atop the castle keep, Rochester Cathedral's splendid spires point towards the heavens. England's second oldest cathedral foundation is only a short walk from the ruined castle.*

**OPPOSITE:** *Now little more than a shell of its original self, Rochester's great keep provided a stalwart refuge for soldiers fighting King's John's army, which failed to pull the mammoth building to the ground.*

# HISTORY

1st century AD – Romans build pharos.

AD 117 – Romans construct fort at the site to base its fleet.

1000 – Anglo-Saxons begin building Church of St Mary-in-Castro.

1066 – William I builds earth-and-timber castle in just eight days; appoints Bishop Odo of Bayeux as constable.

1067 – Count Eustace of Boulogne leads local men in attack on castle.

1180–89 – Henry II erects great keep and other defences and begins underground tunnel network.

1217 – Prince Louis the Dauphin attacks castle with a trebuchet, the first documented use of the siege engine in England.

1220s – Hubert de Burgh, constable and king's Chief Justiciar, extends the outer curtain wall and adds Constable's Gate.

1625 – Inigo Jones refurbishes castle to honour Henrietta Maria of France, Charles I's wife.

1642 – Townsfolk seize castle for Parliament.

Mid-1700s – Systematic clearance of medieval fortifications to make way for modernization in anticipation of attacks by France and Spain.

1780s–1850s – Napoleonic Wars prompt further demolition and addition of new artillery bastions and gun platforms; alteration of underground tunnels.

1803 – 2,000 soldiers occupy underground barracks.

1860s – Church of St Mary-in-Castro rebuilt.

1939 – Vice-Admiral Ramsay uses castle as operations headquarters and lookout, known as Hellfire Corner.

1941 – Construction of an underground hospital.

1956 – Occupation by forces ends.

Early 1960s – Tunnels modernized for government service in the event of a nuclear attack.

1963 – Dover Castle becomes national monument.

1984 – Army decommissions underground installations and turns them over to English Heritage.

# Dover Castle

As early as the 13th century, the chronicler Matthew Paris (*c.* 1200–59) described Dover Castle in Kent as 'Clavis Angliae' – 'the key of England'. The phrase applies as much to the modern site as to its medieval counterpart, for Dover sits just 21 miles (34km) from France, the shortest crossing point between the two nations. The famous port of Dover still welcomes ships from across the English Channel and, nearby, the Channel Tunnel, more often referred to as 'the Chunnel', has eased the journey between England and the Continent.

## The Guardian of England

During most of its lengthy history, Dover has acted as the guardian of England, its fortifications ready to thwart any seaborne invasions. As early as the Iron Age, earthen ramparts defended the hilltop site overlooking the famed White Cliffs. The Romans established a settlement known as Dubris, and their great roadway, Watling Street, started its journey across England to Chester from Dover. To defend Dubris, the Romans erected three stone beacons, individually known as 'pharos', which blazed with fire when warning residents of an imminent attack.

Not to be outdone, the Anglo-Saxons established a 'burh' (a fortified encampment) at Dover, shrewdly extending the Iron Age ramparts to enclose it. The Church of St Mary-in-Castro ('in the castle'), which stands alongside the pharos, marks the location of the ancient settlement. In time, the site received vastly stronger defences, which enabled it to play a crucial role not just in the defence of medieval England but, centuries later, during the Second World War, as the staging point for Operation Dynamo and the evacuation of troops from across the channel in Dunkirk.

## Building Dover Castle

Almost immediately after his victory at the Battle of Hastings in 1066, William I sent troops to Dover to erect a motte castle on top of the Saxon settlement. The symbolism of the effort was certainly not lost on the Norman

OPPOSITE: *Buttressed by a massive inner curtain wall and earthen embankments, the sheer sides of Henry II's great keep at Dover made it virtually impossible to assault on foot.*

BELOW: *Commanding the headland overlooking the English Channel, the castle provided the ideal vantage point for Prime Minister Winston Churchill and Vice-Admiral Bertrand Ramsay to launch Operation Dynamo and the evacuation of Dunkirk in 1940.*

king, nor on the Saxons, whom he had just conquered. Little could William predict, however, that his simple castle would develop into one of England's greatest and most powerful fortresses.

A masterpiece of medieval ingenuity conceived by Henry III's great architect, Maurice the Engineer, Dover's great keep is the classic example of its kind. Rising some 95 feet (29 metres) and crowned with four corner turrets, the heavily defended rectangular tower served as the castle's central strongpoint and the grandiose residence of the reigning monarch. To gain access to the tower, visitors had to pass through the elaborate three-storey forebuilding. The keep's massive stone walls measured between 17 and 21 feet (5 and 6.4 metres) in thickness. They enclosed a well; residential chambers on the first and second floors; the great hall; a state chamber; and the private upper chapel. A mural gallery probably functioned as a fighting platform. The roof level still offers spectacular views of the surrounding urban landscape.

Henry II ringed the keep with a powerful curtain wall, evenly pierced with 10 rectangular towers and two twin-towered gateways. At the northernmost end, the King's Gate opened into a D-shaped barbican, which provided access to the outer bailey and another heavily defended wall of towers and gateways. The barbican also led down into Dover Castle's secret weapon — a network of underground tunnels. Begun by Hubert de Burgh (1165–1243) in the 13th century, and modified for use in modern warfare, the medieval chalk-cut passages still lead to the round St John's Tower and to guard rooms, bombproof passages and the caponier, which crosses the moat at two levels and dates back to the Napoleonic era.

## A Castle Armed

During the late 18th and early 19th centuries, builders worked on an intensive rebuilding project to transform the castle into a sophisticated fortress capable of deploying artillery. Systematically lowering large portions of the medieval curtain wall, troops erected several gun batteries and bastions with underground facilities and caponiers. They also added earthen ramparts to act as obstacles against direct attacks. Later in the 19th century, the walls were fitted with gun emplacements and additional magazines. Each new structure altered

the appearance and military capabilities of the castle, which eventually saw action during the Second World War and the Cold War (1945–90).

## The Realm's Mightiest Castle

Over the thousand years of its existence, Dover Castle has metamorphosed from a primitive earth-and-timber stronghold, which established Norman domination in southern England, into an impregnable concentric castle that projected both symbolic and physical power and challenged anyone, from home or abroad, to pull down its walls. In many ways, Dover Castle is the quintessential medieval castle, yet its strategic value to Britain has persisted well beyond the Middle Ages.

Today, the Lord Warden of Cinque Ports remains the official head of Dover Castle. Until 2002, Queen Elizabeth, the Queen Mother (1900–2002), held this position; however, since her death, the post has remained vacant. English Heritage continues to open the castle to the public, for a fee, throughout the year. Interactive exhibitions occupy portions of the keep and bring to life the drama that made Dover Castle the mightiest castle in the realm.

## HISTORY

1086 – The Domesday Book documents existence of a Saxon hall at the site, held by the Bodehams.

1378 – Sir Edward Dalyngrigge gains possession of the manor of Bodiam by right of marriage to Elizabeth Wardeux.

1483 – Lancastrian owner of Bodiam, Sir Thomas Lewknor of Trotton, forfeits castle and estates to Richard III.

1542 – Sir Roger Lewknor regains full possession of castle and estates.

1639 – Sir John Tufton, 2nd Earl of Thanet and an ardent supporter of the royal cause, reunites manor and castle of Bodiam.

1644 – Tufton sells castle to parliamentarian gunfounder, Nathaniel Powell.

1675 – Elizabeth Clitherow inherits Bodiam Castle upon the death of her husband's father, Sir Nathaniel Powell, 2nd baronet.

1722 – Sir Thomas Webster of Battle Abbey purchases the castle.

1829 – John Fuller of Rosehill purchases castle in order to prevent the Websters from demolishing the site and begins to consolidate the gateways.

1864 – George Cubitt, Lord Ashcombe, begins restoration programme.

1916 – Lord Curzon purchases castle.

1919 – Excavations uncover cannonballs, pottery shards and other artefacts.

1925 – Castle bequeathed to the National Trust.

1930s – The National Trust carries out restoration work.

1970 – Moat is temporarily drained to allow archaeological excavation.

# Bodiam Castle

Walking towards Bodiam Castle in East Sussex is like stepping back in time. Medieval visitors traced the same pathways, weaving and turning along a pre-planned route that was designed to impress and intimidate. Disguised from view by the rolling landscape, the bold towers suddenly burst into view, luring visitors forward in excited anticipation. A spectacle of breath-taking beauty, Bodiam Castle seems to float on top of the shimmering waters of its embracing moat. The visual impact is sheer magic, just as its builder, Sir Edward Dalyngrigge, planned over 700 years ago.

### An Angled Approach
Originally, an unusual series of bridges and paths forced friend and foe to move at angles to reach the gatehouse. This creative design left attackers with their unshielded right sides exposed and vulnerable to retal-iation from inside the castle. It also guided welcome guests around the grand site, directing them to vantage points from where they could appreciate thoroughly Dalyngrigge's architectural prowess and acknowledge his self-importance. Today, the angled bridges no longer exist (except for underwater pilings and the octagonal islet), but their role in protecting and show-casing Dalyngrigge's castle is obvious.

### From Timber to Stone
The threat of a French invasion in 1385 prompted Richard II to grant a licence to crenellate the hall at Bodiam, which required Dalyngrigge to construct a castle capable of defending the locality. Rather than merely fortifying the ageing timber hall, Sir Edward built a new stone castle near the River Rother, from where any attack was likely to occur. Although the final product func-tioned more as an elaborate fortified residence than a heavily defended fortress, the vision of Bodiam Castle rising from the depths of the landscape acted as its primary deterrent to an assault. In any event, the forecasted invasion never took place and the castle's defences were not challenged.

## A Comfortable Castle

An outstanding example of a quadrangular castle, Bodiam is an unexpectedly simple four-sided square, safeguarded by huge circular corner towers and square towers that are posted midway along the east and west walls. Two well-defended gatehouses guarded the northern and southern approaches, and a wooden causeway once bridged the gap between the southern shoreline and the postern gate. Dalyngrigge probably used the southern gateway to transfer supplies and personnel arriving from the Rother across the moat and into the castle.

Valuing comfort over defensive might, Dalyngrigge constructed a series of residential chambers — apartments, a chapel, great hall, kitchen and serving areas and servant's quarters — in logical progression around the inner courtyard. He also provided the officers of the garrison with adequate accommodation that included fireplaces and latrines. The dungeon and guardroom occupied the basement and first floor of the north-west tower, near the main gatehouse.

Dalyngrigge's architect clearly satisfied his employer's requirements for a well-defended stronghold that also paid attention to the personal and private needs of its residents. In all, Bodiam contained 33 fireplaces, 10 spiral staircases and at least 28 latrine chutes. In the aftermath of the English Civil War, Oliver Cromwell's forces slighted the castle, even though it had already passed into the hands of a parliamentarian supporter. Although they

OPPOSITE: *The castle well occupies the entire floor of the basement of the south-west tower. Filled with water from a nearby spring, the 11-foot (3.4-metre) deep well provided an ample supply to the castle.*

BELOW: *Rising from the depths of its water-filled moat, the postern tower provided an alternate entrance into the castle as well as a secondary means of escape. Like the main gatehouse, the southern gateway possessed a variety of defensive devices designed to thwart an assault.*

gutted the interior, the Roundheads left Bodiam's most impressive feature – the towered, moated exterior – almost completely intact.

One of England's most photographed sites, Bodiam Castle honours the memory of its innovative builder, Sir Edward Dalyngrigge. The National Trust opens the site to the public throughout the year for an entrance fee.

ABOVE: *Decorated with heraldic emblems and Sir Edward Dalyngrigge's unicorn crest, Bodiam Castle's great gate-house was protected with three sets of portcullises and heavy timber doors, machicolations, gunports and murder holes.*

LEFT: *Even though the exterior seems perfectly untouched, Bodiam Castle's interiors reveal a different fate – destruction at the hands of parliamentarian forces – which rendered the castle useless, both militarily and residentially.*

# Arundel Castle

The Normans made no mistake when they chose a chalk-laden spur on the River Arun in West Sussex for a castle. William I realized the value of fortifying the spot, which had clear views of the English Channel and allowed easy detection of any inbound French invasion. In 1067, the new king granted the land to Roger de Montgomery, Earl of Shrewsbury (c. 1030–94), who quickly constructed a classic motte and bailey. In time, the stronghold became the seat of the Fitzalans and the Earls of Arundel and of their heirs, the Howard Dukes of Norfolk, who transformed the earth-and-timber castle into the palatial complex we see today.

## A Castle Fit for a Duke

An outstanding example of a motte and bailey that evolved into a substantial stone-enclosure castle, Arundel Castle remains a fitting home for the Dukes of Norfolk, who serve as the highest authority of State on royal ceremonial occasions. Well-preserved Norman zigzag and scrollwork designs distinguish the fine shell keep, which William d'Albini erected in about 1138 to crown the grass-cloaked motte. Inside, the keep still enwraps fireplaces, roof timbers and corbels, features that identify the locations of the hall and sleeping chambers.

ABOVE: *Constructed in the late 19th century, the grand heraldic chimneypiece designed by architect, C.A. Buckler, Surrey Herald Extraordinary, and painstakingly carved by Thomas Earp forms the focal point of the 15th Duke's Drawing Room.*

RIGHT: *Steadfastly safeguarding the north-eastern gateway into Arundel Castle, the Howard lion and Fitzalan horse symbolize the historic link forged between the two families by marriage in 1556.*

Initiating its conversion from a fairly primitive fortification into one of England's greatest treasure houses, Richard Fitzalan, Earl of Arundel (1267–1302), made a lasting mark on the Norman castle. Having endured intensive pounding from parliamentarian cannons mounted on top of the nearby St Nicholas's Collegiate Church in 1642, Fitzalan's twin-towered barbican

## HISTORY

1102 – Henry I besieges castle for three months.

1138 – William d'Albini acquires castle upon marriage to Adeliza de Louvain, Henry I's widow.

1139 – Empress Matilda takes refuge at castle, provoking an attack by King Stephen.

1243 – John Fitzalan, Lord of Clun and Oswestry, acquires Arundel Castle upon marriage to Isabel d'Albini.

1300 – Richard Fitzalan, 1st Earl of Arundel, fights alongside Edward I at Caerlaverock Castle.

1326 – After ordering the beheading of Edmund, 2nd Earl of Arundel, Queen Isabella bestows castle and estates on the Earl of Kent.

1330 – After Kent's execution, Fitzalans regain earldom and castle.

1483 – Richard III creates Sir John Howard as 1st Duke of Norfolk.

1520s–1540s – Thomas Howard, 3rd Duke, introduces his nieces Anne Boleyn and Catherine Howard to Henry VIII, who later marries and then beheads both women.

1572 – Queen Elizabeth orders the execution of Thomas Howard, 4th Duke, for allegedly plotting to marry her rival, Mary, Queen of Scots.

1580 – Philip Howard, grandson of 12th Earl of Arundel and son of 4th Duke, acquires castle, which remains with the Dukes of Norfolk in perpetuity.

1595 – Accused of treason, Philip Howard dies in Tower of London, probably from poisoning.

1642 – Parliamentarian forces desecrate Fitzalan Chapel; after 18 days, royalist constable, Sir Edward Ford, surrenders.

1649 – Parliamentarians slight castle.

1660 – Charles II restores dukedom to the Howards, who also receive the hereditary title of Earls Marshal.

1875–1903 – Henry, 15th Duke, 'Normanizes' castle.

1970 – Philip Howard canonized.

2001 – Edward William Fitzalan-Howard becomes the 18th Duke of Norfolk, Earl of Arundel and Earl Marshal.

RIGHT: *Defended by Robert de Belleme's intimidating twin-towered barbican and the strong inner gateway to the rear, the Norman castle at Arundel challenged all comers to breach its outer defences and storm the massive motte at its core. Even parliamentarian cannon fire during the English Civil War failed to destroy the walls.*

ABOVE: *Restored in 1886, the Fitzalan Chapel features wooden fan vaulting, heraldic emblems, stained-glass windows, lavish sculpted arcades and ornate choir stalls, as well as the family tombs.*

remains one of the castle's oldest surviving structures. This Earl of Arundel also added the Bevis Tower (named for St Bevis), before which statues of heraldic animals – the Howard lion and the Fitzalan horse – proudly stand guard.

Two huge baileys complete the stone-enclosure castle. Named for its reputation as a place for sparring or jousting, the bright green Tiltyard (formerly the outer bailey) is now mainly used for private events. The great Quadrangle encloses the inner bailey with an impressive array of residential buildings, state apartments, a private chapel and the armoury. Designed by English architect C.A. Buckler, each structure contains splendour befitting the realm's premier dukes – and royalty. Stained glass fills windows. Tapestries and family portraits adorn walls decorated with flamboyant chimneypieces. Heraldic

crests rim ornate ceilings. In the Victoria Room, which was named after the Queen's visit in 1846, the fireplace dazzles the senses with lavish carvings, two heraldic flags and a regal shield.

Arundel Castle now resembles a fine art museum laden with historical portraits, grand architectural features and exquisite furniture. Outside, precisely cut stone walls and eye-catching arches hark back to the Middle Ages. Arundel Castle is an exhilarating combination of building periods which reflect the needs of their times and tastes of their owners. Nearby, the historic Fitzalan Chapel contains the ornate tombs of the Earls of Arundel and the Dukes of Norfolk. Today, Arundel Castle Trustees Limited manage the site, and the Dukes of Norfolk continue to live in their ancestral home. It is open to the public during summer months for a fee.

# Corfe Castle

Visible for miles around, the sight of Corfe Castle perched on top of a jutting green hill in Dorset is at once exhilarating and distressing. Golden chunks of giant rock crown the steep-sided hillock, perfectly placed to overawe the countryside. Now embodying the castle's crumbling skeleton, the stones silently and vividly testify to centuries of conflict – and persistence despite the odds.

## The Saxon Succession

In 978, violence erupted at Corfe over the Saxon succession. As the eldest son of King Edgar (959–75), Edward (975–8), had rightfully inherited his father's kingdom on his death, but his stepmother, Elfrida, intended to see her own son, Ethelred (978–1016), planted on the throne of Wessex. On 18 March, 978, King Edward visited his stepbrother at Corfe. According to legend, Edward received a welcome cup of wine from his stepmother upon his arrival. As he drank, Ethelred's retainers stabbed him in the back. Ethelred then began one of the most unsuccessful reigns in British history, gaining the nickname, 'unraed', meaning 'the unready' or ill-advised.

The legend resurfaced a year later, when monks disinterred Edward's bones and found them remarkably intact. They compelled Ethelred to acknowledge his dead half-brother as a saint, and King Edward became known as Edward the Martyr.

## King John at Corfe

During the Magna Carta wars, King John

BELOW: *The embattled remains of medieval Corfe Castle tower above the village where the Saxon King Edward the Martyr reputedly lost his life.*

ABOVE: *A pointed archway still decorates the ground floor of King John's Gloriette, barely hinting at the grandeur of the palatial structure.*

## HISTORY

10th century – Saxons reputedly erect a residence on the north-western corner of the present castle site.

978 – Anglo-Saxon king Edward the Martyr is murdered by his brother's retainers upon his arrival at Corfe. He is later canonised.

1105 – King Henry I erects four-storey, white-washed great keep.

1106 – Henry I imprisons his brother, Robert Duke of Normandy, at the castle.

1139 – King Stephen builds a siege-castle and unsuccessfully assaults Corfe Castle. (The earthworks known as 'the rings' survive just west of the stone castle.)

1204 – King John builds Gloriette and transforms the castle into a palace.

1572 – Queen Elizabeth I, who allegedly detested castles, sells Corfe to Sir Christopher Hatton.

1630s – Sir John Bankes, Lord Chief Justice and loyal royalist, purchases Corfe Castle from the Hattons.

1680s – Sir Ralph Bankes regains custody of the castle after the Restoration, but the family settles at nearby Kingston Lacy.

1981– Mr H.J.R. Bankes places the ruined pile in the care of the National Trust.

ABOVE: *Situated as a stop-gap device between the lower and upper baileys, a masonry wall running between the heavily ruined south-western gatehouse and the forebuilding of the great keep helped prevent access to the bustling core of the castle.*

OPPOSITE ABOVE: *The power of Oliver Cromwell's parliamentarian wrath is vividly represented by the slumping, crumbling round tower that overhangs the western edge of the outer bailey south-east of the great keep.*

OPPOSITE BELOW: *Looking up towards the south-western gate to the great keep beyond, the sheer power of Corfe Castle's curtain wall is obvious, even in its calamitous condition.*

(1199–1216) established his administrative and military headquarters at Corfe, reputedly his favourite residence. The southern half of the boot-shaped castle consists of a large outer bailey enclosed by the towered curtain wall, which was accessed through a twin-towered gatehouse. The wall encompassed the undulating hillside and ended with the great ditch and south-west gatehouse, which defended the summit. Beyond, the west bailey occupies the 'toe' of the boot, which the Normans may have built over an earlier Saxon hall. The 'heel' of the boot commands the highest point of the hilltop site, the inner bailey, which also contained the castle's principal buildings, including the keep.

King John used Corfe Castle as a treasury, prison and royal residence, and embellished the inner bailey with a new palace – the Gloriette. The now jumbled collection of ruined walls and arches belies the Gloriette's original 13th-century splendour, which mainly survives in its details such as foliated ornamentation and pilaster buttressing.

## Corfe and the English Civil War

Corfe Castle's greatest challenge came in the 17th century, during the English Civil War. With the absence of the castle's owner, Sir John Bankes (1589–1644), parliamentary troops readied themselves for an easy victory against the leaderless castle. To delay the inevitable, in May 1643 Lady Mary Bankes wisely signed a treaty agreeing to turn over the castle's four cannons in exchange for her tenants' safety. Meanwhile, she began to stock supplies and recruit aid from supporters of King Charles I.

Two months later, Cromwell's forces began their assault in earnest. For over six weeks, parliamentarian siege engines failed to breach the walls. The attacking army lost over 100 men, but only two royalist soldiers died. When Lady Bankes' loyal husband finally returned to Corfe, he espied what appeared to be the utter devastation of his village and castle. Promptly retreating, the not-so-stout-hearted Sir John abandoned his wife, sons and castle to the machinations of the parliamentarian forces. He died within six months.

Lady Bankes brazenly led her royalist garrison into the fray in 1645. But, in February 1646, one of her own soldiers opened the doors to the besiegers, who swiftly captured the castle. After withstanding seven centuries of tumult, Corfe Castle then met its demise at the hands of parliamentarian troops, who ruthlessly slighted the recalcitrant fortress. Soon afterwards, Lady Bankes moved her children to safety in London.

## A Devastated Site

Today, the towers that protected the western approach to the castle lean precariously over the hillside, separated from the curtain wall; battlements are missing and interiors are mere shells. Inside the castle, the devastation is equally apparent. The massive drum towers that once defended the south-western gateway now stand askew, the western cylinder slumped downhill. Despite the devastation, the ruins persevere, no longer besieged by war engines and defying the debilitating effects of gravity. They buttress one of Dorset's most enchanting structures, mighty Corfe Castle.

Managed by the National Trust, Corfe Castle is open to the public throughout the year for an entrance fee.

# Restormel Castle

## HISTORY

**1086** – Domesday Book records Restormel as part of the manor of Bodardle, held by Turstin the Sheriff.

**1100** – Baldwin FitzTurstin, Sheriff of Cornwall, erects earth-and-timber castle.

**c. 1200** – Robert de Cardinan begins shell keep and gatetower.

**1264** – Simon de Montfort seizes castle from Sir Thomas de Tracy, who had gained possession of the site by right of marriage to Isolda, the de Cardinan heiress.

**1265** – Sir Ralph Arundell takes castle from de Montfort.

**1270** – Isolda de Cardinan grants castle and estates to Richard, Earl of Cornwall.

**1272** – Edmund Plantagenet, Earl of Cornwall, begins major building programme, adds domestic buildings.

**1299** – Earldom and castle revert to Crown.

**1337** – Restormel becomes part of Duchy of Cornwall.

**1354 & 1365** – Edward, the Black Prince and 1st Duke of Cornwall, stays at castle.

**1644** – Royalist troops led by Sir Richard Grenville seize castle and then abandon it.

**1925** – 23rd Duke of Cornwall places decayed castle in State care.

**1984** – English Heritage takes over management of site.

Commanding high land near the western bank of the River Fowey about a mile north of Lostwithiel in Cornwall, Restormel Castle stuns the senses. Protected on three sides by natural slopes and entirely encircled by a 50-foot (15-metre) wide ditch, the deceptively squat site is surely the West Country's most impressive castle. Despite the effects of time and neglect, Restormel Castle remains an outstanding – and unique – example of its kind, an earthen mound crowned with an almost perfectly round shell keep.

### Among the Deer

Erected in the midst of an enormous deer park, Restormel Castle's Norman builders may have originally intended the compact earth-and-timber stronghold to serve as a hunting lodge. By the late 13th century, after its acquisition by the Earls of Cornwall, the site developed from a modest stronghold with timber defences into a fairly secure two-storey stone castle. Its battlemented walls rose 26 feet (8 metres) and measured over 8 feet (2.4 metres) thick. Windows peered outwards only from the upper storey. A substantial gatetower and drawbridge across the moat defended the main entry point. Inside, the formidable slate shell supported the standard buildings expected of any noble castle –

**ABOVE:** *Only the outline of the original fireplace identifies the site of the kitchen block, which filled the area immediately south of the main gatehouse at Restormel Castle.*

**LEFT:** *An unusual arched well chamber projects outward into the inner bailey from the foundations of the solar.*

**OPPOSITE:** *One of the castle's oldest surviving stone structures, the simple square gatetower still serves as the main entrance. It opens into the battlemented shell keep, which traces the perimeter of the steep-sided embankments.*

domestic quarters, latrines, the great hall, kitchen and service chambers. It also surrounded an open courtyard, which offered wandering and work space to the inhabitants. Beyond the solar, or lord's withdrawing chamber, the chapel tower projected outward into the ditch.

## A Triumph of Medieval Engineering

What makes Restormel Castle's shell keep particularly significant is its physical relationship to the earthen mound at its base, which has been characterized both as a motte and as a ringwork castle. Rather than constructing the shell wall around the summit of the mound, which typically occurred when timber keeps were fortified with stone, Robert de Cardinan's workers sank the keep's foundations 6 feet (1.8 metres) down into the earth and cut away a portion of the mound that had originally risen higher. The modifications created the castle's low-lying appearance.

The castle's keepers today speak exuberantly about their favourite site, and rightly so, for the impressive shell keep, grass-covered mound and flat-bottomed ditch vividly demonstrate the talents of medieval engineers, who capably accommodated the domestic needs of castle owners. During the 20th century, the State consolidated the structure to prevent further decay. English Heritage now opens Restormel Castle to the public for an entrance fee, daily from April through to October.

# GREAT CASTLES OF
# SCOTLAND

Scotland's castles chronicle a lengthy and tumultuous history, a heritage marked by Viking invasion, clan strife, the rise and fall of kings — and a notorious queen — and a struggle for independence that spilled over into England. The variation in building style is as dramatic as the geographical differences between the Highlands, Lowlands and Scottish Borders. Masterpieces of baronial splendour, for example Glamis, once the home of Elizabeth Bowes-Lyon, the late Queen Mother, and Dunvegan, which sports the MacLeod Fairy Flag, still house lavish accommodation. Stark tower houses, such as Hermitage Castle, where Mary, Queen of Scots risked her life to care for her ailing lover, and Eilean Donan, the ancestral home of the MacRaes and MacKenzies, stand in everlasting ruin. Defiantly withstanding the terrors of Edward I's war machines, Robert the Bruce's deliberate destruction and the murders of royalty and kinsmen, each left a legacy as vital to Scotland's independence as the blood that was shed on the battlefields at Bannockburn, Flodden Field and Culloden.

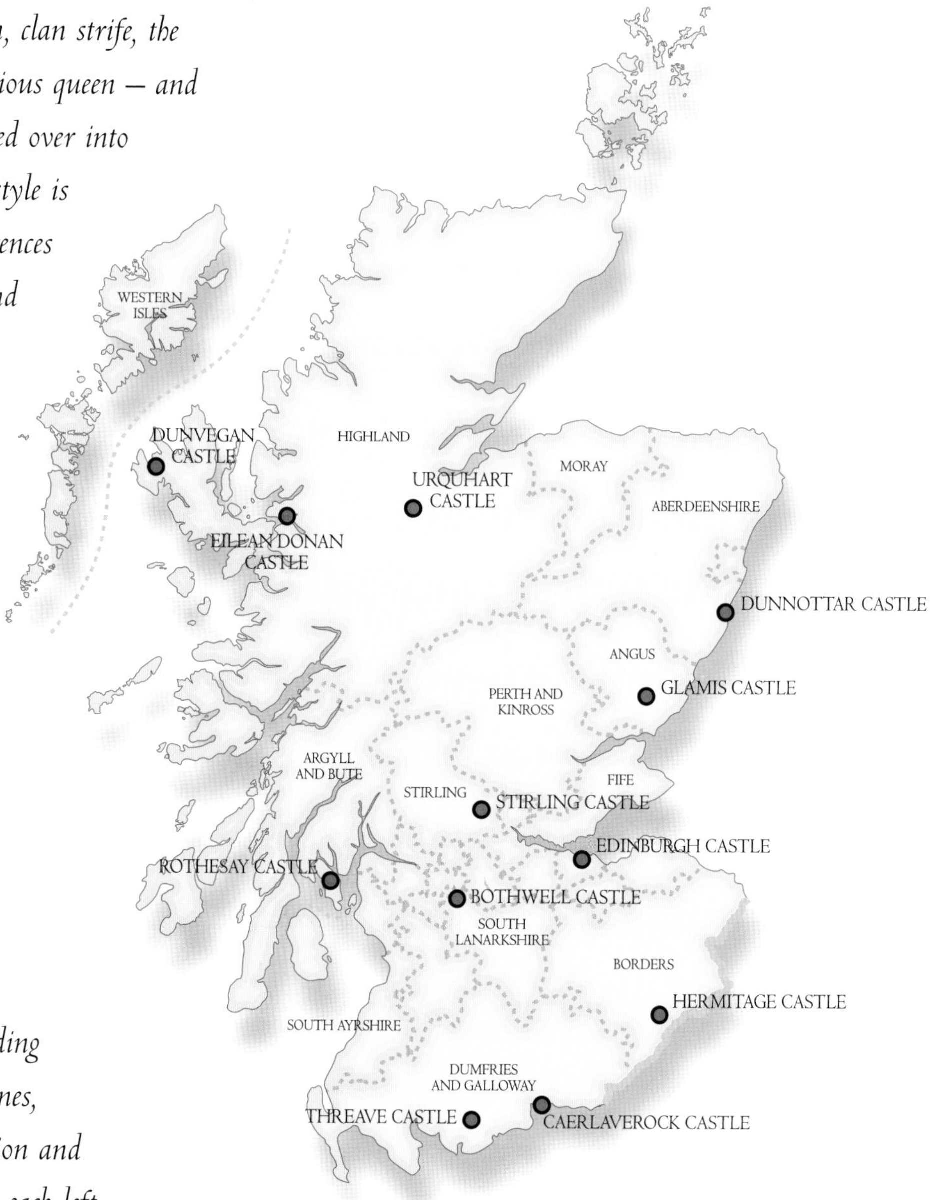

WESTERN ISLES

DUNVEGAN CASTLE

HIGHLAND

URQUHART CASTLE

MORAY

ABERDEENSHIRE

EILEAN DONAN CASTLE

DUNNOTTAR CASTLE

ANGUS

PERTH AND KINROSS

GLAMIS CASTLE

ARGYLL AND BUTE

STIRLING

FIFE

STIRLING CASTLE

EDINBURGH CASTLE

ROTHESAY CASTLE

BOTHWELL CASTLE

SOUTH LANARKSHIRE

BORDERS

HERMITAGE CASTLE

SOUTH AYRSHIRE

DUMFRIES AND GALLOWAY

THREAVE CASTLE

CAERLAVEROCK CASTLE

# Threave Castle

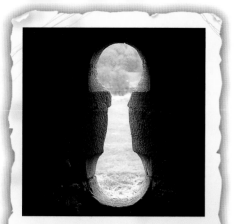

## HISTORY

1369 – Archibald Douglas acquires lordship of Galloway.

1388 – Archibald the Grim, Lord Threave, becomes 3rd Earl of Douglas.

1400 – Archibald the Grim dies at castle.

1447 – Enclosing wall with drum towers and cannon ports is added to castle.

1502 – Casks of red wine and lengths of cloth are purchased in anticipation of a visit by King James IV.

1526 – Maxwells officially appointed as hereditary keepers of Threave Castle.

Mid-16th century – Forces of the Regent Arran control castle.

1639 – Robert Maxwell, 1st Earl of Nithsdale and Lord of Threave, declares support for King Charles I against the Covenanters.

1913 – State acquires castle; archaeological excavations begin.

1970s – Further archaeological excavations undertaken at castle.

Murder, mayhem and Mons Meg dominate the history of a simple tower house perched on an island in the River Dee, near Kirkcudbright. Threave Castle dutifully served the 'Black' Douglases, who used this watery site as a springboard against their rivals, the Stewarts, in the 14th and 15th centuries. As the archetypal Scottish tower house, the stronghold effectively merged simplicity and durability to pose a formidable threat to all comers.

## Galloway's Grim Laird

Archibald the Grim (c. 1328–1400), Lord of Galloway and 3rd Earl of Douglas, erected Threave Castle in 1370 on the site of an earth-and-timber fortification. The illegitimate son and only heir of 'Good' Sir James Douglas (c. 1286–1330), Archibald developed a reputation in Galloway for cold-hearted oppression. Isolated from the surrounding landscape, this inhospitable tower house seems an appropriate home for the despicable Archibald, yet the structure was more elaborate than its severe exterior suggests.

Standing five storeys high, the 8-foot (2.4-metre) thick walls solidly protected the Douglases. Each storey had a specific purpose. Used for storage, the vaulted basement contained the well, a sink and drain and the dungeon. It may also have held servants' quarters. The kitchen level above the basement had a large fireplace, stone sink, deep-recessed window and latrine and probably provided dining space for the servants. A spiral staircase afforded the easy transfer of hot meals between the kitchen and the great hall, purposely located on the floor above. As the laird's showplace, the great hall

*PREVIOUS PAGE: Eilean Donan Castle, near the Isle of Skye, valiantly served the Lords of the Isles, the MacKenzies and MacRaes, and experienced the ravages of clan strife and Viking onslaughts that forged the independent spirit long associated with the Scots. Today, it still evokes awe in the beholder.*

featured an ornate fireplace, three well-lit windows with seats and a latrine. An outside doorway allowed passage between the great hall and boat docks on the river below. Archibald and his descendants lived on the floor above the great hall, the private apartments offering refuge and a bedchamber when guests proved tiring. Meagre accommodation filled the uppermost storey.

## A Bloody Feud

After the death in 1439 of the powerful 5th Earl of Douglas, who was also named Archibald, the relationship between the Black Douglases and the Scottish monarchy, which had never been easy, began to break down. In 1440, the two Douglas heirs, William, the 6th Earl (c. 1423–40), and his younger brother, David, rode to Edinburgh Castle to dine with King James II (1437–60), who was still in his minority. During the 'Black Bull's Dinner', the king's regents, Sir Alexander Livingstone and Sir William Crichton, charged the young Douglases with treason. According to tradition, at the end of the evening's meal, Crichton placed a bull's head before the boys to symbolize their impending

doom. Both were executed in front of the king. Their sister, Margaret, inherited Threave Castle and Archibald the Grim's aged son, James (c. 1371–1443), inherited the earldom. In 1444, Margaret married her cousin, William (c. 1425–52), who became the 8th Earl of Douglas.

The blood feud continued. In 1452, the 8th Earl imprisoned a rival, Sir Patrick MacLellan, who was 'the Tutor of Bombie' and Sheriff of Galloway. Sir Patrick Gray, MacLellan's uncle, visited Douglas, who suspected that Gray carried a release decree for his prisoner signed by the king. Douglas arranged to dine with his visitor before discussing the prisoner's freedom, and during the meal he had MacLellan killed, voiding the orders and enraging King James. The king soon discovered that Douglas was conspiring against him with Alexander Lindsay, Earl of Crawford, and John MacDonald, Lord of the Isles. Allegedly hoping to reconcile the bad blood between them, King James II invited Douglas to dine at Stirling Castle (see pages 79–81). When the 8th Earl refused to renounce his association with Crawford and MacDonald, the king became infuriated and stabbed him to death.

**ABOVE:** *Due to its island location, visitors wanting access to Threave Castle must ring the ferryman for a short ride across the river. The riverside setting posed a significant obstacle to enemy attacks.*

**OPPOSITE ABOVE:** *Soldiers aimed cannons at attackers through the innovative cannon ports that pierced each cylindrical corner tower at Threave Castle. Added in the 15th century to bolster the site's defensive might, they represent the first use of cannon ports in Scotland.*

**OPPOSITE BELOW:** *Viewed from inside the castle courtyard, the fragmentary interior of the ruined tower on the north side of the castle belies the structure's original defensive capacity.*

ABOVE: *Of the four round towers that once guarded the stout tower house, only one survives. Rising to its full height, the three-storey tower withstood King James II's intensive battering in 1455.*

### Defeated by the Mons Meg

In 1455, the king's army defeated James, 9th Earl of Douglas (1426–88), and his assembly of 40,000 men, who had marched to Stirling Castle to avenge the murder of the 8th Earl. Proceeding to Threave, James II scorned the Earl's offer of the castle as a gift and instead erected an artillery wall around the stronghold. The king then bombarded the sturdy tower house with the legendary Mons Meg, which is now housed in Edinburgh Castle (see pages 77–8). Seeing the destruction of several out-buildings, and with their laird safely ensconced in England, the garrison surrendered to the king. From then onward, Threave Castle served as a royal fortress with the Lords Maxwell as hereditary keepers from 1526.

The castle of the Black Douglases faced its final and most devastating siege in 1640, when a force of Covenanters, Calvinist believers determined to enforce Protestant rule in Scotland, wreaked havoc upon the site for 13 weeks. Although left in ruin, the tower house remained strong enough to imprison French prisoners during the Napoleonic Wars at the beginning of the 19th century.

In 1948, the National Trust for Scotland became custodians and started a School for Practical Gardening in the castle grounds. Now under the dual care of the National Trust for Scotland and Historic Scotland, Threave Castle is open during the summer for an entrance fee.

# Caerlaverock Castle

Caerlaverock Castle's blood-red walls rise above the undulating turf like a fiery phoenix protecting its territory. Pronounced in the 14th century by Walter of Exeter as 'so strong that it feared no siege', Scotland's only triangular-shaped fortress is situated in Dumfries and Galloway. It fearlessly withstood five sieges, including a legendary attack by the English monarch Edward I in 1300. Walter, a Franciscan friar, observed and chronicled the entire event in the 'The Song of Caerlaverock'. This fascinating work, which was originally written in French, provides a rare insight into the tactics employed by 'the Hammer of the Scots' to force the unique castle into submission.

## At the Mouth of the River Nith

In the late 13th century, Sir Herbert de Maxwell realized the potency of building a stronghold near the mouth of the River Nith and the tidal waters of the Solway Firth. He constructed a multi-towered stone fortress to replace an earthwork fortification, the remains of which are now obscured by trees just south of the red castle.

Girded by marshland and water-filled ditches, de Maxwell's rust-hued fortress seems to float on the moat's glistening surface. The great twin-towered gatehouse still challenges any assault, its drawbridge and heavy timber doors poised to respond to any affront. Massive cylinders topped with machicolations once defended the two corners of the stronghold; now only Murdoch's Tower survives to its full extent.

The triangular design effectively covered all bases, and shielded the Maxwells from imminent danger.

ABOVE: *Triangular tympana adorned with heraldic and mythological carvings mirror the castle's overall layout. This carving appears on the monumental apartment complex known as the Nithsdale Lodging, which the Earl of Nithsdale built in 1634.*

LEFT: *The castle's twin-towered gatehouse dominates the spot, symbolizing the power of the Lords Maxwell while also posing a formidable obstacle to attack. Grooves used to manoeuvre the drawbridge rise alongside the two round, machicolated gatetowers.*

## HISTORY

**1220s** – John de Muccuswell (Maxwell) builds earthwork castle on estates at Caerlaverock.

**1300** – After partially destroying the castle, Edward I of England appoints Sir Eustace Maxwell as constable.

**1312** – Caerlaverock's constable switches allegiance to Robert the Bruce; the castle endures assault by the English. When Robert orders the dismantling of Scotland's castles to prevent commandeering by the English, Maxwell complies at Caerlaverock.

**1340s** – Addition of Murdoch's Tower.

**1356** – Scots recapture castle from Edward III.

**1425** – Imprisonment of Murdoch Stewart, 2nd Duke of Albany and Regent of Scotland; James, Albany's son, murders the Red Stewart of Dundonald; soldiers transfer Albany and sons to Stirling Castle, where James I orders their execution, but frees Caerlaverock's Lord Maxwell.

**1460** – Robert, 2nd Lord Maxwell, completes castle.

**1545** – Temporarily surrenders to Henry VIII of England, but castle is later taken back by the Scots.

**1572** – English recapture and partly dismantle castle.

**1593** – Addition of gunports.

**1634** – Robert, 1st Earl of Nithsdale, models new apartments on Linlithgow Palace.

**1640** – Castle falls to Covenanters after 13-week siege; Maxwells abandon site in favour of new seat at Terregles; they later move to Traquair House.

**1946** – Duke of Norfolk places castle into State care.

ABOVE: *Building his new apartment complex over a series of barrel-vaulted rooms at basement level, the 1st Earl of Nithsdale made certain to have a reliable and ample supply of drinking water. One of the large chambers contained the wellhead, which probably dates to the 13th century.*

OPPOSITE: *The construction of the Nithsdale Apartments transformed the castle into a luxurious residence, which emphasized the triumph of Renaissance splendour over the militarization of the Middle Ages. Even in ruins, the carved façade reveals the lost grandeur of Caerlaverock Castle.*

### Edward Attacks

For a time, Caerlaverock Castle provided an ideal obstacle to seaborne movement into the Scottish Borders just south of Dumfries. It also played a key role during the wars for Scottish Independence in the late 13th and 14th centuries. Intent on suppressing the Scots, Edward I ordered England's noblemen to assemble at Carlisle for a march against the border castle. Seizure would ease passage between the two countries and allow the king to continue his offensive apace. At Caerlaverock, the army set up camp, erected tents and huts, stabled the horses and foraged for timber and essential resources. Specialist labourers busied themselves building siege engines – a cat, battering ram, belfry, springalds and trebuchets. They also stockpiled boulders, bolts, animal hides and tools.

At the king's command, soldiers scrambled across earthen outworks and water-laden moats and charged the heavily defended gatehouse. Despite several deaths, the castle's defenders remained defiant. After 24 hours of relentless pounding, England's siege machines finally breached the curtain wall. Waving a white flag, the Scots signalled a truce, but swiftly surrendered when the besiegers slaughtered their messenger. Flying Edward I's standard overhead, the English formally seized Caerlaverock Castle. Inside, they encountered only 60 men. Some were freed and others executed.

The Maxwells repaired the damaged castle and occupied the site for another three centuries, switching their allegiance between the Scots and the English several times.

### Renaissance Courtyard

Stepping into the inner courtyard, visitors experience a sudden shift from the military façade of the Middle Ages to the extravagance of the Renaissance. Shield-like tympana, triangular

shapes decorated with mythological scenes and heraldic emblems, frame the windows of the stunning Nithsdale Apartments. Despite their fragility, the intemperate weather and the destructive rage of the Covenanters, the 17th-century movement formed to defend Scottish Protestantism, the carvings are amazingly well preserved. Today, a wing of the castle constructed in the 17th century stands empty, a shell of its former glory. Even so, the red-walled courtyard glows like the most radiant sun.

Today, Caerlaverock Castle is managed by Historic Scotland, and it is open to visitors throughout the year for a small entrance fee.

# HISTORY

**1180** – Walter de Bolbeck, lord of the manor, grants the hermitage and the Church of St Mary to Brother William, a monk from Kelso Abbey.

**1242** – Historic documents record the construction of a castle that almost caused a war between Scotland and England. Scholars associate the site with Hermitage Castle.

**1290** – The death of Sir Richard Knout (Knut) of Keilder, Sheriff of Northumberland, reputedly gives rise to the legend of Cout of Keilder.

**1300** – Castle repaired by Edward I during Wars of Independence.

***c.* 1320** – Robert I grants castle to Sir John Graham, whose son-in-law, Sir William Douglas, acquires the castle by right of marriage to the Graham heiress.

**1335** – Scots monarch Edward Balliol grants castle to English nobleman Ralph Neville.

**1491** – James IV orders Douglas, Earl of Angus, to exchange castle for lordship and castle of Bothwell, held by Patrick Hepburn.

**1540** – Crown annexes lordship of Liddesdale and castle, which is fitted for artillery.

**1587** – James VI grants Hermitage Castle to Francis Stewart, James Hepburn's nephew.

**1594** – Francis Stewart, 5th Earl of Bothwell, attainted; castle and lordship of Liddesdale revert to Crown and then pass to Scotts of Buccleugh.

**18th century** – Masons discover Sir Alexander Ramsay's remains and present them to Sir Walter Scott.

**1820** – Duke of Buccleugh repairs castle.

**1900** – Hawick Archaeological Society excavates chapel site.

**1930** – Castle placed in State care.

# Hermitage Castle

Visitors cannot help having an emotional reaction to Hermitage Castle. Even the novelist Sir Walter Scott (1771–1832) admired the building, favouring it over all other castles. Impressive, oppressive, mournful, forbidding and grim are just some of the adjectives writers have used to describe Liddesdale's imposing fortress. Isolated in the stark, windswept landscape of the Scottish Borders, the hulking block of stone forever guards a low bluff above Hermitage Water. Its severe, tomb-like exterior displays a strength that is capable of withstanding the hostile environment. Targeted by both the Scots and the English, Hermitage Castle has endured the chaos that plagued the border region and fused history with legend.

## A Savage History

As early as the 1240s, an earth-and-timber castle overlooked the boundary that separated wild Scotland from roaming English armies. Possibly erected by the volatile de Soulis family, hereditary butlers to the Scottish king, the early castle no longer survives. However, stories about the cruelty of this Norman family transcend time. Battling a giant warrior, named Cout of Keilder, an early Lord de Soulis watched the slaughter of his subjects before ordering survivors to seize the behemoth. Ensnaring Cout, they hauled the weighty killer to Hermitage Water, where they drowned him in the 'Cout of Keilder Pool'. The men then turned their anger on de Soulis. Binding the laird with ropes and encasing him in lead, they dragged their prisoner to a stone circle named Nine Stane Rig, where they plunged him into a cauldron filled with boiling water.

After the grisly murder, the de Soulis castle passed to Sir William Douglas (*c.* 1300–53) in 1338. Acclaimed as the Knight of Liddesdale and the Flower of Chivalry, Douglas also had a savage side. In 1342, he seized his nemesis, Sir Alexander Ramsay, who was praying at St Mary's Church in Hawick, and threw him into the dungeon at Hermitage Castle. Ramsay managed to survive for 17 days, feeding on bits of grain that fell from the floor above. The dungeon pit in the north-east tower probably served as Ramsay's jail.

In 1353, William, the 1st Earl of Douglas (*c.* 1327–84), murdered his namesake and kinsman in Ettrick Forest and, for a time, controlled Hermitage Castle. In 1358, the Dacres acquired the castle by right of marriage to Sir William's widow and replaced the stronghold with a fortified dwelling. The oldest example of English domestic work in Scotland, the building's red sandstone remnants survive in the fabric of the later castle.

## H-Shaped Fortress

Regaining possession in 1371, the Douglases converted Hermitage Castle into a dour L-plan tower house and added three enormous towers to the unprotected corners. Each tower held well-apportioned

**ABOVE:** *Approaching Hermitage Castle from the south-west, visitors can imagine the tower house's H-shape. The western façade features a row of large rectangular doors at roofline, which once gave access to a timber hoard or fighting platform.*

**OPPOSITE:** *Restored during the 19th century, the enormous pointed flying arch penetrating the eastern face of the tower house is one of the castle's most distinctive features and heightens the sense of foreboding that radiates from its walls.*

RIGHT: *Named for Brother William, a hermit who settled here in the late 12th century, Hermitage Chapel served the nearby castle. Today, only foundations survive, along with a small cemetery, about 200 yards (180 metres) from Hermitage Castle.*

BELOW: *Stone projections, known as corbels, once supported the timber beams that held the floors together. Their placement shows the height of each storey inside the empty castle.*

latrines, which dumped into basement cesspits that drained into the moat and flushed the waste into Hermitage Water. With the construction of a fourth, bulkier angle tower in 1400, the Douglas castle acquired its final, H-shaped form. Arguably the castle's most distinguishing feature, the flying arches distributed the massive weight of the corner towers across the façades to prevent collapse.

## A Scandalous Liaison

In October 1566, the border reiver (raider) Little Jock Elliot gravely injured James Hepburn, 4th Earl of Bothwell (1536–78). For days, Hepburn writhed in pain at Hermitage Castle. News of Bothwell's injuries quickly travelled the 40 miles (64km) to Jedburgh, where Mary, Queen of Scots (1542–87) was holding court. Despite the impropriety – both were married to other people – and still recovering from childbirth, Mary risked her life and the Scottish monarchy to visit her failing lover. Returning to Jedburgh the same night, Mary fell seriously ill. For 10 days, she lay perilously close to death. Years later, after Bothwell's treachery and her interminable months of imprisonment, Mary often lamented, 'Would that I had died at Jedburgh'.

Visitors to the castle have reportedly seen the ghostly figures of Mary, Sir Alexander Ramsay and Lord de Soulis, whose victims reputedly shriek from the torture inflicted upon them. Historic Scotland opens Hermitage Castle for an entrance fee during the summer months.

# Edinburgh Castle

Over the course of its historic past, Edinburgh Castle has functioned as a royal residence, a military citadel and store for royal artillery, a treasury, a prison and a repository for the Scottish government's records. Its location on a giant volcanic plateau carved by glacial ice flows high above the city gave the castle strength, status and command over the region. Perched on Castle Hill, at the upper end of Edinburgh's Royal Mile, the heavily militarized castle provides a stark contrast to the Palace of Holyroodhouse, the spacious official residence of the Scottish monarch at the opposite end of the Royal Mile.

## A Great Military Heritage

Edinburgh Castle is a living tribute to Scotland's great military heritage. The upper bailey is home to both the ornate Scottish National War Memorial – one of its newest buildings – and humble St Margaret's Chapel, its oldest surviving building. The

ABOVE: *Regimental bagpipers perform amid a row of cannons poised along the battlements.*

BELOW: *Gazing at Edinburgh Castle from Prince's Street Gardens, one can easily imagine the intimidating effect created by the mass of stone and bedrock from its lofty position well above the enemy's heads.*

## HISTORY

AD 638 – Angles capture Din Eidyn, a fort erected by the Celtic Votadini tribe, and anglicize name to Edinburgh.

1093 – Queen Margaret dies at Edinburgh after receiving news of deaths of King Malcolm and one of their sons.

1124 – David I begins castle's transformation into royal fortress; erects St Margaret's Chapel, which he dedicates to his mother.

1296 – Edward I captures castle after a three-day siege.

1313 – Scots retake castle and demolish defences on Robert the Bruce's orders.

1356 – David II begins major rebuilding effort.

1440 – The 'Black Dinner': Earl of Douglas and his young brother are killed in presence of king.

1482 – Scottish nobles briefly imprison James III at castle.

1571–73 – The Lang Siege: garrisoned for Mary, Queen of Scots, the castle is besieged for two years before surrendering.

1570s–80s – Artillery defences erected.

1633 – Charles I stays overnight.

1640 – Convenanters seize castle after three-month siege.

1650 – Oliver Cromwell establishes his Scottish headquarters at castle.

1685 – Archibald, 9th Earl of Argyle, is imprisoned in castle.

1689 – Jacobite supporters forced to surrender castle to supporters of William III.

1715 – Jacobites assault castle.

1745 – Prince Charles Edward Stuart storms Edinburgh, but fails to take castle.

1763 – Imprisonment of French soldiers.

1829 – Mons Meg returns to castle from Tower of London.

1846 – St Margaret's Chapel is rediscovered.

1861 – One O'Clock Gun fired from castle for first time.

1923 – Last use of castle as a prison.

1996 – Stone of Destiny returns to Scotland.

**ABOVE:** *Pipe and drum bands gather together on the esplanade for the finale of the Edinburgh Military Tattoo, staged since 1950 at the historic castle.*

Queen Anne Barracks, the Great Hall and the Palace and Crown Square remain the royal heart of the castle. The buildings have been altered over time, but the medieval antecedents remain, largely hidden underground or incorporated within the fabric of later structures.

## A Royal Residence

Built by James IV (1488–1513) in the early 16th century, but restored in the late 19th century, the Great Hall features an elaborate hammer-beamed roof, a faithful replica of the original. Another remarkable feature of the hall is a series of subterranean barrel-vaulted tunnels, which were built to support the weight of the structures overhead. Having held prisoners in the late 18th century, the vaults now make room for mighty Mons Meg, the mammoth cannon presented by the Duke of Burgundy to James II in 1457 and put to such effective use at Threave Castle (see pages 68–70).

At the eastern end of the Great Hall, James IV built a new palace to provide accommodation for the resident monarch. Like the other buildings enclosing Crown Square, the Palace has been modified several times by successors to the throne, and now presents a façade that chills rather than welcomes.

In 1566, Mary, Queen of Scots gave birth to the future King James VI (1587–1625) inside the stylish Queen's Bedchamber. In 1707, the palace stalwartly safeguarded the Honours of Scotland – the Crown, Sceptre and Sword of State – which went on display after their rediscovery by Sir Walter Scott in 1818. Today, another of the nation's most historic treasures, the Stone of Destiny, occupies a place of honour alongside the crown jewels of Scotland.

## A Military Establishment

By the 1650s, Edinburgh Castle had primarily become a military establishment, and remains so to this day. New fortifications, for example Butts, Argyle and Dury's Batteries, reflect the Army's increasing focus on heavy artillery, while the addition of the military prison, governor's house and hospital fulfilled security, residential and medical requirements. The old hospital and ordnance storehouse now contain the National War Museum of Scotland. The castle serves as headquarters for the Scottish Division, the Royal Scots Regiment and the Royal Scots Dragoon Guards, who garrison the site.

Historic Scotland manages Edinburgh Castle, which is open daily throughout the year for an entrance fee.

# Stirling Castle

It is no mere coincidence that Stirling Castle, raised on a bed of volcanic rock, became Scotland's primary medieval fortress, for it controlled passage between north and south and access to the sea. Coveted by the English and favoured by the Stewart (Stuart) kings, who spent more time there than at any of their other fortresses, this stalwart stronghold endured siege after siege and the continual changing of owners, and dutifully served its countrymen well into the 20th century. Not only does the site deserve the moniker 'the key to Scotland', in many ways Stirling also deserves recognition as Scotland's greatest castle.

## Command and Defiance

A fortress of some sort – probably built with earth and timber – stood on top of the rocky plateau as early as the 12th century, but much of the assortment of buildings that now dominates the site dates no earlier than the 15th century. The castle's substantial defences – the curtain wall, forework, numerous modern fortifications and two large baileys – enclose four royal buildings. Together, they create the clear impression of noble dominance, as if the castle had erupted from the bedrock to command the region.

Stirling played a critical role during the Scottish Wars of Independence. In 1304, the besieged garrison stalwartly resisted Edward I's best efforts to

**ABOVE:** *Completed for the christening of James VI's infant son in 1594, the Chapel Royal features a decorative western wall, painted in anticipation of a visit by Charles I in 1633.*

**LEFT:** *Reopened by Queen Elizabeth II in 1999, James IV's lavish Great Hall now features an elaborate hammer-beam ceiling and an unusual limewash exterior.*

## HISTORY

AD 842 – Kenneth MacAlpin, King of the Scots, reputedly besieges the site.

1174 – Treaty of Falaise: in exchange for freedom, William I (the Lion) gives control of key Scottish castles to England's Henry II.

1189 – Richard I returns castle to William the Lion.

1291 – Scots swear fealty to Edward I at castle.

1297 – Scots recover castle after William Wallace's victory over the English at Stirling Bridge.

1298 – Edward I regains control after his victory at Falkirk.

1314 – After the Battle of Bannockburn, Robert I orders the castle's destruction to prevent English recapture.

1333 – English troops begin rebuilding programme.

1343 – Robert Stewart captures castle.

1425 – Execution of Duke of Albany and sons.

1439 – Queen Joan becomes castle prisoner, two years after seeking refuge there.

1452 – James II murders William, 8th Earl of Douglas, at castle.

1513 – Queen Margaret Tudor seeks shelter after Battle of Flodden; two-year old James V is crowned in chapel royal.

1543 – The infant Mary, Queen of Scots is crowned in chapel royal.

1567 – Mary sees James for the last time at castle; three months later, he becomes king.

1594 – During James VI's sensational banquet in the Great Hall, a huge wooden ship fires 36 brass cannons.

1650 – Parliamentarian troops besiege castle.

1689–1714 – Addition of artillery batteries and gun emplacements.

1715 – Headquarters for Duke of Argyll during Jacobite Rising.

1746 – Castle artillery defeats Jacobites, led by Bonnie Prince Charlie.

18th and 19th centuries – Refitted for artillery.

1849 – Queen Victoria visits Stirling Castle.

1996 – Chapel Royal restoration concludes.

pull down the walls. Their defiance so enraged Edward that, when the 30 defenders finally offered surrender after two months of bombardment, starvation and exhaustion, Edward ignored the white flag. Instead, he chose to demonstrate his omnipotence before accepting the garrison's submission. Ordering his men to erect a giant trebuchet, a siege engine nicknamed 'Warwolf' for its ability to strike fear into the hearts of intended victims, Edward I wreaked havoc on the castle and savoured the Scots' humiliation.

**BELOW:** *Restored after a devastating fire in 1855, the King's Old Building stands on the castle's highest point and overlooks the charming knot garden in the flatlands below.*

## Stirling and the Stewart Kings

Almost two centuries after Edward I hammered the Scots, James IV initiated the first extensive building programme at the royal fortress. His achievements include the King's House (now known as the King's Old Building), the forework and the great hall, which recently reopened to the public after receiving a somewhat controversial facelift.

Now glowing with bright limewash, the brilliance of Scotland's largest great hall, which measures 138 by 47 feet (42 by 14.3 metres), is

impossible to avoid. Heated by five great fireplaces, lit by two giant bay windows and several smaller lights, equipped with four turnpike staircases and adorned with conical turrets and ornate carvings, this stunning building provided the ideal setting not only for kings to confer with Parliament, but also for feasting and celebrations.

Begun only 20 years after the great hall, the lavish palace constructed by James V (1513–42) was intended to impress his second wife, Mary of Guise (1515–60), whom he had married in 1538. Bedecked with an array of sculpted creatures, gods and goddesses and even a carved portrait of the king, the Renaissance exterior is the palace's most impressive feature. Inside, the palace contained private and official chambers for the monarch. Besides the bedchamber, the king's lodgings contained two public rooms for receiving guests and conducting the affairs of State. Of particular note, the panelled ceiling of the royal presence chamber once featured carved oak roundels, the 'Stirling Heads', which presently hang on the walls after one of them fell onto a bystander in 1777. For his queen, James V added a similar suite of rooms, which included a guard room, the queen's presence chamber and a bedchamber.

During the 16th century and later in the 18th and 19th centuries, Stirling Castle advanced from the age of the siege engines into the age of artillery. In 1559, when Mary of Guise ordered the construction of the French Spur, the castle still largely served as a royal residence. In 1603, after the accession of James VI as James I of England, the primary royal stronghold and the focus of the Scottish monarchy shifted to England. From then on, Stirling Castle functioned principally as a military establishment and the outer perimeter acquired a variety of gun batteries, magazines, barracks and casemates.

Finally released by the Army in the 1960s, Stirling Castle is now maintained by Historic Scotland. It is open to the public throughout the year for an entrance fee. The recently restored Chapel Royal and Great Hall honour Scotland's historic past, when Stirling Castle, under the Stewart monarchy, played a key role in controlling the kingdom and ensuring its ongoing freedom.

BELOW: *Guarding the lowest fording point on the River Forth, Stirling Castle dominates its surroundings from its location atop a bed of sheer-sided volcanic rock. From this spot, people have witnessed the clashes of cultures for well over a millennium.*

## HISTORY

1242 – Walter de Moray (Moravia) inherits estates; begins castle.

1270s – William 'the Rich' Moray, Lord of Bothwell, fortifies the castle in stone.

1296 – English capture castle; William Moray dies.

1297 – Moray's heir, Andrew, dies during Battle of Stirling Bridge.

1299 – Scots capture castle after 14-month siege.

1301 – Edward I and an army of 7,000 soldiers retake castle; Aymer de Valence, Earl of Pembroke and Warden of Scotland, acquires castle and barony of Bothwell.

1314 – Scots partly demolish castle, pushing a portion of the keep into River Clyde.

1336 – Edward III establishes headquarters at Bothwell.

1337 – Led by Sir Andrew Moray, rightful owner and Warden of Scotland, the Scots ravage castle.

1362 – Archibald 'the Grim', 3rd Earl of Douglas and Lord of Galloway, acquires castle by right of marriage to Joanna Moray and initiates rebuilding programme.

1455 – James, 2nd Lord Crichton, obtains castle upon Douglas forfeiture.

1484 – Castle passes to Sir John Ramsay of Balmain.

1489 – Patrick Hepburn, 2nd Lord Hailes and later Earl of Bothwell, acquires castle.

1492– Hepburn exchanges Bothwell for Hermitage Castle, held by Red Douglases, Earls of Angus.

1584 – Dame Margaret Maxwell, Countess of Angus, surrenders castle to the Crown.

1669 – Archibald Douglas, 1st Earl of Forfar, acquires castle; pulls down part of the structure to construct mansion.

19th century – Earls of Home acquire castle.

1926 – Forfar mansion demolished.

1935 – Earl of Home places castle in State care.

# Bothwell Castle

Taking its inspiration from the great French donjon at Coucy, which was destroyed in 1916, ruined Bothwell Castle in Lanarkshire remains Scotland's greatest 13th-century stone-enclosure castle. Dominated by the massive 90-foot (27.4-metre) high cylindrical keep, the red sandstone fortress guards a bend in the River Clyde south-east of Glasgow. Intended as a polygonal stronghold fronted by a twin-towered gatehouse and defended with massive round towers, much of the stone castle never saw the light of day. Even so, the contrasting red walls and green landscape dazzle the eyes.

### The Tallest Round Keep

Enclosed with 15-foot (4.6-metre) thick walls and protected by a 15-foot (4.6-metre) deep ditch spanned by a drawbridge, Scotland's tallest round keep gallantly served its owners not just as the castle's strongpoint, but also as its finest residence. Featuring a vaulted basement, which was primarily used for storage; a 20-foot (6-metre) deep well; a first-floor hall; second-storey quarters for soldiers or retainers; and an upper level fitted with the lord's private apartments, a latrine and access to the wall-walk, the keep offered a large degree of comfort and symbolic status. A turnpike staircase connected the levels, while an expanse of curtain wall linked the keep first to a smaller postern tower, which allowed escape during a siege, and then to the battlemented prison tower.

Still rising its full height, the prison tower overlooks the striking remains of an elaborate hall that was probably begun in the 15th century, but which was

ABOVE: *Having played a central role in the Wars of Scottish Independence, Bothwell Castle endured repeated sieges by the Scots and English. The well-preserved machicolated South Tower demonstrates the physical power that gave the castle its strategic value.*

LEFT: *Cleverly placed latrines deposit outside the castle walls next to the ruined prison tower.*

not completed until the following century. Now little more than a shell, the hall originally featured an ornate dais-end window, a minstrel's gallery, fireplaces and a spiral staircase, which allowed access to the first-floor chapel.

**An Incomplete Castle**
Besieged time after time, Scottish and English owners barely had the chance to repair any damage before the next onslaught took place. Concentrating primarily on the southern half of the site, they erected a rectangular enclosure, which was defended by the donjon and two round towers. Yet, they neglected the northern side, where the gatehouse, another round tower,

two latrine turrets and the remainder of the curtain wall should have stood. Although successive owners undoubtedly spent a fortune tending to the castle, builders never fully completed Bothwell Castle before financial coffers emptied.

Regardless, what survives honours the engineering skills of its medieval designers, who strove to erect the land's finest donjon. Once completed, the reddened walls and round towers would certainly have rivalled other castles in contemporary Europe. Even in ruin, the majestic splendour of the original castle enlivens the site.

Historic Scotland maintains Bothwell Castle for the State; it is open throughout the year for an entrance fee.

ABOVE: *Even when viewed from inside the castle, Scotland's tallest round keep dominates the western end of the pentagonal courtyard. Sadly, much of its exterior was demolished after the Battle of Bannockburn (1314) and pushed into the River Clyde.*

## HISTORY

**1098** – Norse king, Magnus Barefoot, erects moated earth-and-timber stronghold.

**1204** – Alan, 2nd High Steward, builds St Michael's Chapel.

**1263** – Battle of Largs: Scots defeat Vikings and regain control of castle.

**1360** – John Stewart, Robert II's son, becomes hereditary keeper of Rothesay.

**1401** – Robert III creates his son as Duke of Rothesay; title passes in perpetuity to the eldest sons of the kings of Scotland.

**1406** – Robert III dies at castle.

**1462** – Earl of Ross attacks castle.

**1498** – Butes become hereditary keepers.

**1527** – Master of Ruthven attacks castle.

**1544** – Earl of Lennox captures castle for England.

**1659** – Parliamentarians slight castle.

**1685** – Argyll Highlanders burn castle.

**1816** – 2nd Marquess of Bute begins repairs.

**1870s** – 3rd Marquess implements restoration programme.

**1961** – State takes over care of castle.

# Rothesay Castle

Rising from the depths of an encircling water-filled ditch, Rothesay Castle in Argyll and Bute strains for recognition in a land of baronial splendour. Yet, the distractions of modern buildings, rumbling traffic and the spectacle of more glamorous castles, such as Glamis (see pages 86–7) and Dunvegan (see pages 95–7), have not diminished the historic importance of this impressive early masonry stronghold. Despite the simple design, Rothesay Castle fearlessly endured Viking, Scottish and English assaults to become a favourite residence of the Stewart kings.

### Nordic Heritage

As early as 1204, Alan, 2nd High Steward of Scotland, began the castle's transformation from a primitive earth-and-timber fortress into a surprisingly strong fighting machine. Now, thanks to the efforts of the Marquesses of Bute, Stewarts by blood, who dredged the moat and made essential repairs, the compact stronghold retains its structural integrity.

Also known as a castle of 'enceinte', Rothesay features a circular curtain wall, which smartly traced the shape of the supporting mound and formed a fine shell keep. Equipped with arrow slits and defended by four strategically placed towers, the 10-foot (3-metre) thick battlemented walls offered tremendous protection to castle inhabitants.

The earliest documented castle at Rothesay appears in *Haakon Haakonson's Saga*, an epic poem written in about 1230. According to the saga, Uspak, a Norse chieftain also known as Husbac, commanded 80 Viking ships in an assault against the stronghold. The battle was bloody, as the garrison inside the castle used molten lead and boiling pitch to drench the attackers. In response, the Norsemen manned a siege tower, battered the walls with powerful timber rams and employed miners to tunnel beneath the foundations. After three days, the unusually resilient castle fell to the invaders, who had hacked their way through the walls and then slaughtered the 390 Scottish defenders.

### The Stewart Gatehouse

Rothesay's four-storey gatehouse, which was begun by James IV in the 15th century and completed by James V about a century later, is structurally similar to the L-shaped tower house that appeared throughout Scotland at about this time. Its long, vaulted passage not only provided access to the inner courtyard, but also linked to the adjoining porter's lodgings, the guard room and a postern gate, which led to the moat. A trap-door in the floor of the passageway opened into a dank dungeon pit, which plunged well below ground level. The first floor held a substantial great hall measuring 49 feet in length and about 25 feet (7.6 by 15 metres) in width, a large fireplace and the laird's solar. Upper storeys functioned as private quarters, and their latrines deposited into the moat below. Two adjacent towers housed the garrison.

Today, Rothesay Castle, one of Scotland's earliest stone fortresses, is managed by Historic Scotland and is open throughout the year for an entrance fee.

OPPOSITE ABOVE: *A cannon aims across the water-filled moat at Rothesay Castle, daring anyone to breach the serenity.*

OPPOSITE BELOW: *Providing the castle's main living quarters, the great gatehouse at Rothesay contained the great hall, lord's solar, bedrooms, a pit prison and latrine chutes, which emptied into the moat below.*

BELOW: *The L-shaped main gatehouse juts into the waters of the encompassing moat at Rothesay Castle. On the grass-covered platform to the rear, one of four stout round towers projects outward from the original shell keep.*

# HISTORY

**8th century AD** – Irish cleric, St Fergus, establishes a cell at the site.

**1034** – Malcolm II dies at Glamis after battle on Hunter's Hill.

**1234** – Documents record Glamis as a thanage.

**1372** – Sir John Lyon of Forteviot acquires thanage and inherits royal hunting lodge.

**1376** – Robert II re-designates Glamis as a feudal barony and grants it to Sir John Lyon, Princess Joanna's husband.

**1377** – Lyon becomes Chamberlain of Scotland.

**1382** – Sir James Lindsay of Crawford murders Lyon in his bed.

**1445** – Patrick Lyon becomes 1st Lord Glamis.

**1537** – King James V condemns Lady Glamis for treason and witchcraft; she is burned at the stake near Edinburgh Castle.

**1537–42** – James V and Mary of Guise hold court at castle.

**1562** – Mary, Queen of Scots stays overnight at Glamis.

**1575–1615** – Patrick, 9th Lord Glamis, remodels castle.

**1606** – James VI and I creates Patrick as 1st Earl of Kinghorne.

**1715** – Charles, 6th Earl, entertains James VIII (the Old Pretender), who uses touch to cure sufferers of 'King's Evil' (scrofula).

**1767** – John, 9th Earl, weds Mary Eleanor Bowes, daughter of George Bowes of Streatlam Castle.

**1773** – 9th Earl of Strathmore remodels castle.

**19th century** – John, 10th Earl, acquires title Lord Bowes; he later changes his surname to Bowes-Lyon.

**1914** – Glamis serves as a hospice during First World War.

**1923** – Lady Elizabeth Bowes-Lyon, youngest daughter of 14th Earl, weds Prince Albert, Duke of York.

**1930** – Princess Margaret Rose is born at castle.

**1936** – Lady Elizabeth Bowes-Lyon becomes Queen Elizabeth; Prince Albert is crowned as King George VI.

# Glamis Castle

'This castle hath a pleasant seat; the air nimbly and sweetly recommends itself unto our gentle senses.' So William Shakespeare described Glamis, the legendary setting for one of his best-known tragedies, *Macbeth* (*c.* 1606). Yet, even though it is unlikely that the bard ever visited the castle in Angus, his description reflects accurately the opinion of one of its owners – Patrick Lyon, 9th Lord Glamis and 1st Earl of Kinghorne (*c.* 1578–1616), who allegedly met Shakespeare while he was penning the historic play for James I. A more modest structure in Shakespeare's day, the palatial tower house has capably served monarchs and nobility – including the long-standing Lyon family – for over 700 years. Its pointed turrets and slender, symmetrical windows pull one's eyes toward the heavens, from where the late Queen Mother surely gazes down upon her ancestral home.

### A Simple Hunting Lodge

Originating in the 14th century as a simple royal hunting lodge, the first Glamis Castle probably consisted of a small building, a few ancillary structures and a courtyard enclosed with a timber palisade and moat. Over time, the site quickly developed into an imposing stronghold, its 8-foot (2.4-metre) thick walls absorbing the earlier structure. During the early 15th century, the Lyons replaced the timber defences with a barmkin, or stone curtain wall, and improved the outbuildings. By the 1440s, the addition of the main tower gave the castle its L-shaped plan.

## A Stately Residence

During the 17th century, the aforementioned Patrick Lyon added three vaulted storeys to the central tower, capped them with conical turrets and bartizans and built a round tower on either end of the wings. In the angle of the 'L' at the junction of the two main wings, the 1st Earl of Kinghorne also erected the unusual stair tower, which rises 143 steps from the basement up to the battlements.

The kitchen, servants' quarters and stores filled the ground floor. The first floor featured a lesser hall, the great hall dominated the second storey and private apartments occupied the top level. Later in the same century, the 3rd Earl of Kinghorne, another Patrick Lyon (1643–95), tore down much of his namesake's work, and transformed the red castle into the extravagant marvel that dominates the lush estate.

Today, Glamis Castle overflows with memorabilia, fine artwork, tapestries and furnishings, ornate plasterwork ceilings, heraldic emblems and lavish chimneypieces. As the stately residence of the Earls of Strathmore and Kinghorne, the magnificent building both honours its ancient past and fulfils splendidly its current role as one of Scotland's greatest — and most eye-catching — treasures. Glamis is open daily from late March to early October and an entrance fee is charged.

**ABOVE:** *Statues of King Charles I and King James VI gaze with perpetual admiration at the grand spectacle of Glamis Castle.*

**RIGHT:** *Originally used as the great hall, the enormous drawing room now features a stunning array of royal portraits. The lavish chimneypiece and the arched plasterwork ceiling were added in the early 17th century.*

**OPPOSITE ABOVE:** *The central stair tower rises skyward between the castle's two main wings.*

**OPPOSITE:** *The barrel-vaulted crypt at Glamis Castle dates to the 14th century, when it served as the lower hall and provided a dining area for the household. It reputedly contains a secret chamber.*

## HISTORY

**5th century AD** – St Ninian establishes church at site.

**900** – Vikings slay King Donald II at Dunnottar.

**1296** – William Wallace captures castle and reputedly burns to death 4,000 English soldiers.

**1336** – Edward III seizes castle, which Sir Andrew de Moray, Scottish Regent, retakes and devastates.

**1382** – Sir William Keith, Great Marischal of Scotland, exchanges Struthers in Fife for Dunnottar lands, then owned by William Lindsay, Lord of the Byres.

**1562 and 1564** – Mary, Queen of Scots stays overnight at Dunnottar.

**1580** – James VI meets with Privy Council at castle.

**1595** – Dunnottar becomes the venue for the burning of witches.

**1639** – William Keith, 7th Earl Marischal, declares support for Covenanters.

**1645** – James Graham, Marquis of Montrose, besieges castle and burns surrounding estates.

**1651** – King Charles II uses castle to safe-guard Scottish crown jewels; the wives of George Ogilvy (the castle governor) and Reverend Grainger (a local minister) and a kinswoman of Lady Ogilvy's hide the regalia.

**1652** – After an eight-month-long siege, the starving garrison surrenders to parliamentarian troops, who fail to recover crown jewels.

**1685** – 167 Covenanters are held in appalling conditions in 'Whigs' Vault'.

**1689** – Castle becomes a Jacobite prison.

**1715** – George, 10th and last Earl Marischal, forfeits castle after participating in failed Jacobite rebellion.

**1718** – Dismantling of castle.

**1727** – Keiths reacquire castle and estates, which they retain until 1873.

**1925** – Annie, 1st Viscountess Cowdray, begins restoration project.

**1990** – Mel Gibson makes a film adaptation of William Shakespeare's *Hamlet* at castle.

# Dunnottar Castle

Declared on a 16th-century Privy Seal as 'one of the principal strengths of the realm', Dunnottar Castle in Aberdeenshire did not acquire such a fitting description solely from the power of its location. The comment also honoured the status of its owners, the Keiths, Earls Marischal of Scotland from the 14th century to the 18th century. As hereditary commanders of the Scottish cavalry, the earls played a key role in Scottish politics over the centuries. Their great fortress, now a massive ruin, dominates a flat-topped peninsula linked to the shore by a thin strip of land. Its sheer cliffs drop abruptly to the North Sea, 160 feet (48.8 metres) below.

### Securing Scotland's Honours

Perfectly poised to watch over both land and sea, Dunnottar Castle occupied one of Scotland's most magnificent defensive sites. The strength of the mighty fortress was so widely recognized that, in 1651, King Charles II (1660–85) chose Dunnottar Castle to store his state papers and the Honours of Scotland – the Crown, Sceptre and Sword of State – to prevent them from falling into parliamentarian hands during the Civil War. The shrewd thinking of three courageous women thwarted English efforts to seize the items. Smuggling the regalia past Cromwellian troops, they placed the goods underneath the floors of the Kirk of Kinneff, where they remained safely hidden from view for almost a decade, only to see the light of day once more after the Restoration.

## Construction and Covenanters

An expansive stone-enclosure castle covering over 3 acres (1.2 hectares) of land, Dunnottar is still dominated by the sturdy L-plan tower house that was begun by William Keith in the late 14th century. A fine example of its kind, the battlemented tower house rose for four storeys, held a prison and storage area in the basement; a great hall on the first floor; an upper hall and the laird's private rooms on the second level; and bedchambers above. Servants' quarters probably filled the space underneath the garret.

The 4th Earl Marischal, known as William o' the Tower, added several noteworthy buildings at Dunnottar. For his son and new daughter-in-law, William built a huge courtyard house, known as Waterton's Lodging, which he surrounded with several ranges of buildings, including a great hall and private apartments, a long gallery, chapel, forge, barracks and stables. Altogether, the new accommodation displayed in a much more grandiose way — at least to

William's thinking — the trappings of a family of such high status. One can only imagine the 4th Earl's horror had he known that, in 1685, Dunnottar Castle would become a death-trap and torture chamber for Covenanter prisoners, who refused to concede the king's authority in religious matters. Nine of the prisoners died there during what was an extremely hot summer.

The castle's perilous and dramatic position created the perfect setting for the turmoil it witnessed over the centuries of its existence. No longer the setting for vicious acts of persecution, Dunnottar Castle's cluster of ruins perseveres against the devastating effects of rain, wind and saltwater. Today's visitors can still experience the intensity of the place, which served as the seat of the Keiths, welcomed kings and queens and endured the tumult that has characterized so much of Scotland's past.

Dunnottar Castle is managed by the Dunecht Estates Office and is open daily from Easter to October for a fee.

**ABOVE:** *Dunnottar Castle's classic L-plan tower house dominates the ruins of the cliff-top site.*

**OPPOSITE ABOVE:** *To cross between the mainland and the headland jutting into the North Sea, castle builders shrewdly cut a tunnel, which could be blocked to thwart the enemy, into the rocky strip between them.*

**OPPOSITE BELOW:** *During the unusually hot summer of 1685, 122 Covenanter men and 45 women were packed into the castle's stifling prison, known as the Whigs' Vault. Nine prisoners died, while another 25 managed to escape.*

# HISTORY

**12th century** – William the Lion reputedly builds earth-and-timber castle.

**1229** – Alan Durward, Alexander II's son-in-law, acquires lordship of Urquhart; begins stone castle.

**1252** – King accuses Durward of treason; the Comyns acquire castle.

**1296** – Edward I batters castle with siege engines, appoints William Fitzwarine as constable.

**1297** – Scots recapture castle; Sir Alexander de Forbes becomes constable.

**1303** – Edward I retakes castle, appoints Sir Alexander Comyn of Badenoch as constable.

**1308** – Robert the Bruce grants castle to Sir Thomas Randolph, later Earl of Moray.

**1333** – Constable Sir Robert Lauder thwarts English siege.

**1346** – Ownership of Urquhart reverts to monarchy.

**1437** – Alexander MacDonald, Earl of Ross and Lord of the Isles, captures castle.

**1476** – Castle passes to George Gordon, 2nd Earl of Huntly.

**1513** – Donald MacDonald of Lochalsh, Lord of the Isles, captures castle.

**1545** – MacDonalds and Camerons of Lochiel lay waste to castle and surrounding area.

**1644** – Covenanters plunder castle; Lady Urquhart retains possession.

**1689** – Grant Highlanders withstand Jacobite onslaught, but castle begins to decay.

**1692** – Castle is slighted.

**1715** – A great storm devastates castle; tower house collapses.

**1912** – Castle passes to the State, who prohibit quarrying at the site.

**1977** – Loch Ness Monster reportedly sighted from castle.

# Urquhart Castle

Poised on the tip of a sandstone ridge jutting into Loch Ness, Britain's deepest freshwater loch, Urquhart Castle receives swarms of visitors hunting the famed monster. Yet, the hourglass-shaped castle was not built to seek the elusive creature. Rather, its position at the junction of the Great Glen and Glen Urquhart gave owners control of a vital communications route through the Scottish Highlands. Today, the dramatic ruins only hint at the castle's original strength, but testify steadfastly to its historical significance.

For centuries, the stronghold at Strone Point capably served Scottish kings and clan commanders, enduring boldly siege after siege to become one of the land's most evocative visions. Even when English armies managed to capture the site, the Scots rapidly took back their castle. Simple in plan, Urquhart Castle featured two enclosures, the walls of which traced the perimeter of the promontory and supported the castle's most important domestic structures, the great hall, kitchen block and great chamber.

### The King's Grant

The castle's crowning glory is its four-storey tower house. Modified in stages from the 14th through to the 17th centuries, the rectangular tower dominates the north-eastern tip of the site. The main building period probably dates to 1509, when King

James IV bestowed the lordship of Glen Urquhart on John Grant of Freuchie, the 'Red Bard'. The king required Grant to add a tower, an outwork of stone and lime, a hall, a kitchen and other facilities, including a pantry, a brewhouse, a bakehouse, an oxhouse, a dovecote and a kiln. Of these buildings, mostly foundations remain, but the corn kiln exists in fine condition inside the gatehouse.

Urquhart Castle's strategically positioned twin-towered gatehouse had 10–12-foot (3–3.7-metre) thick walls, small watch-rooms in the corner turrets and residential chambers fitted with fireplaces, latrines and closets.

Originally defended with a portcullis, heavy timber doors and murder holes, the gate passage, massive walls and round towers posed a formidable obstacle to an assault. Nearby, the rock-cut ditch handily defended the inland side of the castle, from where an enemy most likely would stage an invasion.

## Commanding Castle

After the construction of the Caledonian Canal at the southern end of Loch Ness, the waters rose over 6 feet (1.8 metres) yet failed to diminish the castle's command of the landscape. Despite siege, slighting, storm damage and throngs of visitors seeking the elusive Nessie, the fine enclosure castle has endured staunchly the passage of time, and the views of Loch Ness and the splendour of the castle ruins will not fail to tantalize your senses. Now in the care of Historic Scotland, who have recently opened a new visitor centre, Urquhart Castle is open throughout the year for a fee.

ABOVE: *The approach to Urquhart Castle plunges downhill towards Loch Ness. Some scholars believe the Picts occupied a fort here long before any castle was built.*

OPPOSITE ABOVE: *Urquhart Castle maintains its positional advantage at the centre of the Great Glen.*

OPPOSITE BELOW: *Only the lower levels of the twin-towered gatehouse survive. Inside one of the round towers, the remains of a corn kiln suggest a past domestic use.*

# Eilean Donan Castle

## HISTORY

1220 – Alexander II builds castle in response to Viking threat.

1263 – Alexander III grants castle to MacKenzie ancestor Colin Fitzgerald, son of Ireland's Earl of Desmond and Kildare, for service at the Battle of Largs.

1306 – John MacKenzie shelters Robert the Bruce.

1331 – Randolph, Earl of Moray and Warden of Scotland, executes 50 local men and displays their heads on the battlements.

1509 – MacRaes become hereditary constables.

1539 – Donald MacRae uses his last arrow to kill Donald Gorm, claimant to Lordship of the Isles.

1654 – Scottish parliamentarians burn castle.

1719 – English troops destroy castle.

1912–32 – Lt.-Col. John MacRae-Gilstrap rebuilds castle.

1955 – Castle opens to the public.

1983 – Establishment of Conchra Charitable Trust.

1984 – Castle provides setting for Highlander movie.

1990s – Interiors renovated, furnished and opened to the public.

During the early 14th century, the MacRaes of Cluns fostered Mary, daughter of the last chief of the Bissets. Upon her marriage into Clan Fraser, Mary brought the estates of the lordship of Lovat to her husband's family. Afterwards, she honoured her upbringing and affection for her foster parents by placing a stone over the entrance to Beaufort Castle. The Gaelic inscription read: 'As long as a Fraser lives within, let not a MacRath (MacRae) remain without'. Six hundred years later, when the MacRaes restored their ancestral stronghold on St Donan's island, they installed a similar plaque. It says (in Gaelic): 'As long as there is a MacRae inside, there will never be a Fraser outside'. The motto not only celebrates the abiding relationship between the two clans, but also displays the strength of MacRae ties to the region.

## Guardian of the Lochs

Shrouded more days than not with mist and cool breezes, Eilean Donan Castle is wrapped with romance and stunning scenery. Dominating an islet at the head of Loch Duish, Scotland's most photographed castle was ideally positioned to guard the Kyle of Lochalsh at the point where lochs Duich, Long and Alsh converge south-east of the Isle of Skye.

Linked historically to Abbot Donan, a 6th-century Celtic saint who reputedly founded a small cell at the spot, the name translates as 'island of Donan'. Late in the 13th century, Kenneth MacKenzie controlled the castle, which served as the clan seat for 300 years. Serving as MacKenzie bodyguards, the MacRaes acquired the nickname 'MacKenzie Shirt of Mail' and became hereditary constables of the castle in the early 16th century. In many ways, Eilean Donan Castle is more a reflection of the status of the MacRaes in the region than that of the MacKenzies.

## Attacked from the Sea

Over time, succeeding owners altered the stone castle, actually reducing it in size while enhancing its defensive prowess. During the Jacobite Rising of 1719, three English frigates, HMS *Worcester*, HMS *Enterprise* and HMS *Flamborough*, bombarded Eilean Donan Castle, which William MacKenzie, 5th Earl of Seaforth, had garrisoned with Spanish troops. Upon discovering over 300 barrels of gunpowder inside the defiant defences, the English set them alight and blasted the castle into pieces.

## The Castle Recreated

What we see today is a superb, albeit mostly 20th-century, recreation of the original castle of 'enceinte', and the walled courtyard always protected the three-storey 14th-century tower house. After having a vision, Farquhar MacRae encouraged Lt.-Col. John MacRae-Gilstrap to spend over £230,000 to transform the tumble-down ruins into a castle resembling the structure he had imagined.

Crowned with crow-stepped gables, the tower house featured corner turrets, a barrel-vaulted basement and a great hall on the first floor. The top level contained bedrooms linked to the lower floors by a staircase turret. MacRae-Gilstrap also added a stone bridge, which visitors may use to reach the island even when the castle itself is closed. Curiously, just before they completed work on the new castle, the men

OPPOSITE: *The MacRae heraldic crest displays red stars, red lions and a right hand grasping a sword or scimitar. It occupies a place of honour above a series of clan shields decorating the flamboyant chimney piece in the banqueting hall.*

BELOW: *Farquhar MacRae's castellated vision, reflected in the waters of Loch Duich, sits upon an islet named for St Donan, a Celtic hermit who settled in the shadow of the mountains of Skye in the 7th century AD.*

discovered plans for Eilean Donan dating to 1714, which had long been stored at Edinburgh Castle. The designs matched almost exactly the images Farquhar had seen in his dreams.

As trustees of the Conchra Charitable Trust, descendants of Lt.-Col. John MacRae-Gilstrap continue to revitalize Eilean Donan Castle so that future generations can carry on the family's proud traditions and go on living in their ancestral home. The trust opens the castle daily from April to November and it can be visited for a fee.

LEFT: *Banquet preparations are made by the Lady of the castle, the butler and scullery maids in this realistically refurbished kitchen.*

BELOW: *Once the site of the great hall, the restored banqueting hall features historical items and furniture, and transports visitors back to the Middle Ages, when the chamber served as the castle's entertainment centre.*

# Dunvegan Castle

Dunvegan Castle's owner, John MacLeod, the 29th chief of the MacLeod clan, touts his home as 'the jewel in the crown of the Isle of Skye', and rightly so. Having housed 20 generations of chiefs, the castle is Scotland's oldest continuously inhabited structure. Bounded on three sides by treacherous cliffs and loch waters and protected on the fourth side by a deep-cut ditch, this stunning stronghold is rich in scenery, history, folklore, architectural splendour and precious artefacts.

### A Castle in Disguise

Having undergone at least nine major rebuilding phases, the present castle little resembles its medieval precursor and may

ABOVE: *Bonnie Prince Charlie's well-preserved waistcoat is on display inside the MacLeod castle.*
BELOW: *The Library at Dunvegan Castle boasts a fine portrait of a Lady of MacLeod.*

## HISTORY

Early 13th century – Leod, a Norse prince and the clan's progenitor, occupies castle of 'enceinte'.

14th century – Malcolm, the 3rd MacLeod chief, reputedly slays a rampaging bull as he returns home from visiting his lover, the wife of Fraser of Glenelg.

1500 – Alasdair Crotach erects Fairy Tower; founds College of Pipers for the MacCrimmons, the MacLeods' hereditary pipers.

17th century – Rory (Ruaridh) Mor, 15th chief, adds long hall to Fairy Tower.

17th century – Ian Breac, 18th chief, rebuilds Rory Mor's house at castle.

1773 – James Boswell and Dr Samuel Johnson visit castle.

1790 – Great keep reroofed.

1815 – Sham gatehouse constructed.

1840–50 – Castle undergoes extensive restoration programme.

1851 – Norman MacLeod, 25th chief, leaves castle after potato famine bankrupts him and takes a clerk's job in London to support his family.

1929 – Reginald MacLeod, the 27th MacLeod chief, returns to live at Dunvegan Castle.

1933 – Castle opens to public access.

be more accurately classified as a grand stately home. However, fragments of the original castle, including the great keep, survive, disguised beneath the pepperpot domes and other 19th-century accoutrements. The modifications in effect transformed Dunvegan Castle into a lavish L-plan castle, dominated by the Fairy Tower and several ranges of buildings, a long gallery, the barracks block and Rory Mor's hall.

## A Clan Protected

Dunvegan Castle's most priceless gem, the centuries-old Fairy Flag (Am Bratach Sith, in Gaelic), hangs in the tower constructed by Alasdair Crotach ('Crouch-backed'), the 8th MacLeod chief. Endowed with magical powers, the Fairy Flag safeguards the clan – but only if unfurled on three occasions. According to legend, Alasdair used the flag's magic twice, so the MacLeods have one last chance to profit from its powers.

How the Fairy Flag made its way to Dunvegan Castle remains a mystery. One story claims that, upon Harald Hardrada's defeat by the Saxons in 1066, a MacLeod ancestor, Godred Crovan, seized the flag from the Norsemen and carried it to Scotland. Another version contends that, in the 14th century, the 4th chief claimed the flag as booty from battle. Tradition also has it that couples placing the banner on their bed will ensure their fertility. Some maintain that the flag can entice herrings into Loch Dunvegan.

The Fairy Flag may have helped Clan MacLeod avoid disaster in the mid-16th century when Iain Dubh, a man of questionable character, schemed to become chief. Having already murdered his half-brother, the clan's rightful heir, Dubh hunted down the three remaining obstacles to his inheritance – his half-nephews. Spotting the boys and their tutor as they entered Dunvegan Castle, Dubh slammed down the portcullis, isolated the boys from the rest of their company and massacred them.

Unaware of the travesty, Mary, Queen of Scots sent 11 Campbell clansmen to the Isle of Skye to assess Dubh's fitness to become chief. After learning that Dubh had welcomed the

*BELOW: Refurbished in the late 18th century, the simple furnishings of the Drawing Room belie the chamber's original grandeur and uncomfortable location near the castle's dungeon. Among its treasures are paintings of the 23rd Chief and his second wife, Sarah.*

Campbells with a lavish banquet – complete with blood disguised as red wine – and then murdered her emissaries, Mary and the Campbell Earl of Argyll set out to avenge the deaths. Iain Dubh fled to Ireland, where he soon offended the Irish O'Donnells, who disembowelled the Scot with red-hot pokers. Norman MacLeod, the legitimate heir, returned to Dunvegan Castle as clan chief. The Fairy Flag had kept its promise.

## 'HOLD FAST'

Perhaps the Fairy Flag has already depleted its magic, having been unfurled on other occasions. In 1799, a mischievous servant reputedly freed the flag during the absence of the 23rd chief. At the moment of unfurling, the warship on which the MacLeods' son served was destroyed at sea. The presence of the flag was also unable to prevent the 25th chief from bankrupting himself to provide for the needs of his clansmen during the 1846 Potato Famine; he eventually sold the castle's riches and rented it out to raise money.

Despite these setbacks, Clan MacLeod, the castle, the Fairy Flag and its legends persevere. In 1938, Dunvegan Castle caught fire. As the castle burned, residents carried treasures, including the Fairy Flag, to safety. According to legend, as the flag passed the blaze, the flames cooled and the inferno extinguished itself. Five years later, during the Second World War, MacLeod airmen so strongly believed in the power of the flag that they wore replicas underneath their jackets while flying missions against the Germans.

Magic, folklore and intrigue have melded into reality at Dunvegan Castle. Besides the Fairy Flag, visitors may view the bull's horn retrieved by Malcolm, the 3rd chief, after slaying the animal with a dirk. Each male heir traditionally demonstrates his manhood by drinking claret from the horn. Fancifully restored during the 19th century, Dunvegan Castle's battlemented towers fittingly convey Clan MacLeod's motto: 'HOLD FAST'. The castle is open throughout the year for a fee.

**ABOVE:** *Known in Gaelic as 'Dun Bheagan', the castle's romantic reflection dates to the late 19th century, when Robert Brown the Younger of Edinburgh redesigned the stronghold to show off the tastes of the 25th Chief of MacLeod.*

# GREAT CASTLES OF
# WALES

'Nowhere in these islands does the splendour fall more generously than on the castles of Wales', observed the late Wynford Vaughan-Thomas, historian, writer and broadcaster. Indeed, castles survive in virtually every town or village in Wales. They may not resemble imposing stone fortresses such as Raglan, but, at the very least, they include earth-and-timber castles, for example Twthill near Rhuddlan. As World Heritage Sites, Edward I's Conwy, Caernarfon, Harlech and Beaumaris castles have achieved international renown for their 'outstanding value to humanity'. Yet others, like White and Kidwelly Castles, deserve greater recognition for their physical strength, or for innovative architectural features, as at Pembroke, where the great donjon has no parallel. In a nation renowned for its unrivalled density of castles, the splendour of which ranges from Welsh-built simplicity at Dolwyddelan to Caerphilly, one of medieval Britain's most complex fortresses, Wales can properly claim the title 'Land of Castles'.

ISLE OF ANGLESEY
BEAUMARIS CASTLE
CONWY CASTLE
RHUDDLAN CASTLE
CAERNARFON CASTLE
CONWY
FLINTSHIRE
DENBIGHSHIRE
DOLWYDDELAN CASTLE
WREXHAM
HARLECH CASTLE
GWYNEDD
CEREDIGION
POWYS
PEMBROKESHIRE
CARMARTHENSHIRE
WHITE CASTLE
KIDWELLY CASTLE
RAGLAN CASTLE
PEMBROKE CASTLE
NEATH PORT TALBOT
RHONDDA CYNON TAFF
CAERPHILLY
MONMOUTHSHIRE
SWANSEA
CAERPHILLY CASTLE
NEWPORT
CHEPSTOW CASTLE
BRIDGEND
CARDIFF
VALE OF GLAMORGAN

# HISTORY

1060s – William FitzOsbern builds earth-and-timber castle at the site.

1138 – King Stephen unites the Three Castles into a single lordship.

1186 – Ralph of Grosmont supervises construction of stone keep and curtain wall.

1201 – King John grants lordship and castles to Hubert de Burgh.

1205 – William de Braose, Lord of Abergavenny, acquires lordship.

1254 – Three Castles granted to Lord Edward, the future King Edward I.

1257 – Demolition of great keep.

1267 – Edmund 'Crouchback', Earl of Lancaster and Edward's brother, receives White Castle.

1538 – Castle documented as roofless and extensively decayed.

1825 – Duke of Beaufort purchases castle from Duchy of Lancaster.

1902 – Beaufort sells castle to Sir Henry Mather Jackson.

1920s –- State takes over care of castle.

1960s – German prisoner of war, Rudolf Hess, visits castle to feed swans.

# White Castle

One's first impression of Monmouthshire's White Castle marries awe with disbelief. Situated in the midst of verdant fields, enduring hedgerows and a scattering of well-kept homes, the stone fortress seems almost out of place. Yet, admirers have long described White Castle in Llantilio as 'the dreamer's fairy-tale castle'. And rightly so, for this masonry masterpiece possesses all the features anyone would expect from a medieval stronghold — a huge twin-towered gatehouse preceded by a wooden bridge, sitting astride a grassy mound, encircled by a deep, water-filled moat and commanding sweeping vistas of the countryside. During the Middle Ages, the effect would have dazzled the eyes, for the castle received its name from its white plaster walls, which must have gleamed on sun-filled days.

## Good Defences

Even in ruin, the castle of Llantilio conveys power and stability. Although it centred a large manorial estate, White Castle served chiefly as a military base rather than a regal residence. Henry II initiated the castle's transition from a primitive earth-and-timber fortification into a well-defended fortress during the 1180s. Remodelling the stronghold using a design typical of the

ABOVE: *Surrounded by a water-filled moat and a sturdy stone wall, White Castle's outer bailey acted as a first line of defence should an assault occur.*
PREVIOUS PAGE: *Edward I's mighty Conwy Castle has achieved its status as a World Heritage Site for being one of Wales' most magnificent fortresses.*

OPPOSITE: *Presenting an image of power and grace, identical drum towers dominate the main gatehouse at White Castle.*
BELOW: *With views as far as distant Pen-y-Fan in the Brecon Beacons, the hilltop upon which White Castle stands was an ideal setting for a castle.*

**ABOVE:** *Now a mere shell of its original self, the inner bailey contained all the domestic comforts a resident would need, including the ever-essential well.*

once, losing his castles repeatedly and making only minor repairs to the castle of Llantilio. On de Burgh's death in 1243, Henry III granted the three castles to his sons, Edward and Edmund, as lords in their own right. They initiated the major building programme that transformed the fairly basic castle into a fairy-tale fortress.

During the rebuilding campaign, not only was the main gate turned into a postern gate, but the entire focus of the castle shifted 180 degrees to the north. Builders added two new gate-houses to the northern defences and attached four drum towers to the 12th-century curtain wall. When finished, the castle of Llantilio featured three complementary sections: an outer bailey enclosed by a dry ditch and towered curtain wall and fronted with its own gateway; the inner, moated castle with its massive towers, intimidating gatehouse and domestic buildings; and the hornwork, which provided a barrier to unwanted access from the south.

## Sister Castles

The best way to experience White Castle is to first explore its architecturally simpler sister castles at Skenfrith and Grosmont. Then, ascend the narrow, undulating lanes to the massive Marcher castle near Llantilio Crossenny. Wander the outer bailey. Imagine scores of soldiers setting up tents and stabling horses as they did centuries ago. Climb to the top of the gatehouse and enjoy panoramic views of the undulating landscape. Visualize the vanished buildings and ruined towers completely rebuilt, plastered a lustrous white and prepared to serve their lords. Even as an empty shell, White Castle can change dreams into reality.

White Castle is maintained by Cadw, and is open throughout the year; a fee is charged during the summer.

times, Ralph of Grosmont supervised the construction of a square keep and stone curtain wall. A simple gateway alongside the keep served as the main entry point. Anyone wanting access had to cross the hornwork, a crescent-shaped chunk of land enclosed by water, to enter the castle.

## Fairy-Tale Fortress

Although frequently granted to loyal subjects, White Castle remained predominantly a royal stronghold. During the early 13th century, Hubert de Burgh, King John's justiciar, controlled White Castle and its sister fortresses at Skenfrith and Grosmont. De Burgh fell in and out of the king's good graces more than

# Raglan Castle

Erected late in the history of medieval castle building, Raglan Castle proclaims itself proudly as the last castle to withstand a parliamentarian battering during the English Civil War. Commanding a Monmouthshire hill close to the border with England, this flamboyant castle remains a refreshing vision in the lush surrounding countryside. In its heyday, Raglan Castle easily tolerated intensive assaults, enraging the likes of Oliver Cromwell, whose men struggled to pull down its mighty keep. Possessing a delicacy that is reminiscent of Renaissance France, where aesthetics played a crucial role in castle design, the fortress also possessed an interior environment that rivalled any monarch's residence. Indeed, the enchanting structure can rightly claim honour as Wales's most splendid castle.

## French Style

In response to mounting hostilities during the 15th-century Wars of the Roses, Sir William ap Thomas, the Blue Knight of Gwent, erected a huge castle with a double bailey at Raglan. Influenced by the peculiarities of French castles, ap Thomas and his son, William Herbert, implemented a grand scheme featuring hexagonal and semi-hexagonal forms and the prolific use of machicolations.

Sir William's greatest achievement was the Twr Melyn Gwent, or Yellow Tower. Situated on its own, just outside the main walls of the castle, this hexagonal great tower functioned as a self-sufficient structure – a keep capable of withstanding a lengthy siege. Of the five original storeys, only four survive. The basement level, highlighted by its enormous fireplace and fine latrine, contained the kitchen and possibly the treasury. Fireplaces, latrines and progressively larger windows

**ABOVE:** *The worn but still exquisite carvings of two human figures adorn the remains of a fireplace that graced the castle's Long Gallery.*

**LEFT:** *The bulky twin-towered gatehouse provided extra defensive support and also contained elaborate apartments.*

## HISTORY

**1172** – Walter Bloet controls Raglan, part of the lordship of Usk.

**Late 14th century** – Elizabeth Bloet inherits manor of Raglan.

**1432** – Sir William Herbert purchases manor from stepson, James, Lord Berkeley; begins masonry castle.

**1462** – Harri (Henry) Tudor, the future King Henry VII, is raised at Raglan.

**1465** – Raglan becomes a Marcher lordship.

**1468** – Herbert becomes Earl of Pembroke after seizing Harlech Castle.

**1469** – Richard Neville, Earl of Warwick, orders Herbert's execution after Battle of Edgecote.

**1475** – William Herbert acquires castle upon reaching his majority.

**1479** – Edward IV bestows castle upon his son, Edward, Prince of Wales; Herbert receives the earldom of Huntingdon.

**1491** – Sir Walter Herbert manages castle on behalf of Elizabeth Herbert, his niece and rightful heir.

**1508** – Castle passes by right of marriage to Sir Charles Somerset, Baron Herbert of Raglan, Chepstow and Gower.

**1549** – William Somerset, 3rd Earl of Worcester, initiates final building programme and begins formal gardens.

**Early 17th century** – Edward Somerset, 4th Earl, adds water gardens, summer-houses and moat walk.

**1642** – Henry Somerset, 5th Earl and 1st Marquess of Worcester, declares support for Charles I.

**1640s** – Edward Somerset, 2nd Marquess, builds 'water commanding machine'; construction of Civil War fortifications.

**1646** – Parliamentarians erect siegeworks and defeat garrison.

**1660s** – Henry Somerset, 3rd Marquess, acquires castle, which becomes a stone quarry.

**1682** – Somerset becomes Duke of Beaufort.

**1756** – Henry Somerset, 5th Duke of Beaufort, prohibits further quarrying.

**1938** – 10th Duke places castle into State care.

ABOVE: *Even in ruin, the heavy hexagonal walls of the Yellow Tower of Gwent display power and intimidation. Defended at its base with a six-towered masonry wall and a postern gate that allowed access to the moat, the great keep could capably sustain itself during a siege.*

reveal the residential roles of the upper chambers. From the upper storeys, soldiers had clear views of the countryside and the Civil War siegeworks that were constructed near the main gate in the 17th century.

## Resisting the Roundheads

Despite incessant bombardment by parliamentarian troops in the summer of 1646, the great tower of Raglan refused to yield. Realizing that this mighty castle was not going to fall easily, Cromwell's men constructed earthen siegeworks just outside the fortress's walls to support additional cannons and mortars, including the powerful Roaring Meg. With Roaring Meg in place, the Marquess of Worcester recognized the futility of the fight. The royalist garrison

marched away from the castle to the sound of drums and trumpets, with standards waving and their horses and weapons at their sides. Their leader marched away to imprisonment and execution. The castle, however, endured, its great keep steadfastly resisting the efforts of Cromwell's men to demolish it.

## Raglan's Renaissance Garden

Beyond the great gatehouse, keen-eyed observers will identify the tall kitchen tower in the northern corner of the cobbled courtyard. Its dank basement offered cool storage (the wet larder). The buttery and pantry stood immediately to the west, and the great hall occupied the western side of the bailey. Originally embellished with enchanting carvings, a massive fireplace, stained

glass and wood panelling, the hall must have exuded splendour. Above the raised dais, where the lord and his special guests dined, a carved plaque commemorated the 3rd Earl of Worcester's selection to the prestigious Order of the Garter.

Beyond the great hall, apartments dominated the western side of the castle, which was known as the Fountain Court. In addition to the chapel and long gallery, the grand stair, a latrine tower and the South Gate – the castle's original entrance – encircled the Fountain Court. Once acclaimed for its beauty, a graceful fountain stood in the centre of the courtyard. Sadly, only its foundations survive today.

The apron wall encircling the great tower leads to a well-preserved postern gate, a latrine turret and five other turrets, which probably supported cannons. Across the water-filled ditch, the grassy moat walk takes visitors past 15 brick niches, which once held busts of Roman emperors. Lavish terraced gardens added by the Earls of Worcester featured two summerhouses, a bowling green, a great pool, a knot garden and a formal water garden. Now recognized as one of Britain's most important surviving Renaissance gardens, Raglan's fantastic grounds and giant rectangular lake decorated the northern and western sides of the castle.

Even in ruin, majestic Raglan Castle inspires respect and wonderment – and remembers a garrison's courage against a more formidable foe. Managed by Cadw, it is open throughout the year for a fee.

**ABOVE:** *Arguably William Herbert's finest contributions to Raglan Castle, the machicolated great gatehouse and neighbouring hexagonal Closet Tower reflect the influence of stylistic developments in France on British castle-building.*

# Chepstow Castle

## HISTORY

1067 – William FitzOsbern, Earl of Hereford, begins hall-keep.

1071 – Roger de Breteuil inherits castle.

1075 – Castle reverts to monarchy after de Breteuil's failed rebellion.

1115 – Henry I grants castle to the de Clares, Earls of Pembroke.

1176 – Isabel de Clare inherits castle; custody passes to Crown.

1189 – William Marshal, Earl of Pembroke, acquires castle by right of marriage to Isabel de Clare.

Early 13th century – Major rebuilding programme.

1270 – Roger Bigod III, Earl of Norfolk, inherits castle; final rebuilding phase includes town walls.

1306 – Upon Bigod's death, castle reverts to monarchy.

1320s – Hugh le Despenser controls castle.

1403 – Thomas Mowbray, Duke of Norfolk, garrisons castle against Owain Glyndŵr.

16th century – Somersets, Earls of Worcester, make improvements to castle.

1645 – Royalist garrison surrenders to parliamentarians.

1646 – Royalist leader, Sir Nicholas Kemeys, seizes castle, but is forced to surrender to parliamentarians.

1650s – Becomes military barracks and prison; re-fortified against artillery.

1680 – Henry Marten, regicide, dies after 20-year imprisonment at the castle.

1690 – Garrison withdraws.

19th century – Castle becomes a smithy and glass factory.

1953 – Chepstow passes into State care.

Completely occupying a limestone ridge above the River Wye, mighty Chepstow Castle in Monmouthshire commands a strategic river crossing between England and Wales, which is known in Welsh as *Ystraigyl*, or 'the bend in the river'. While effecting their conquest over the Saxons, the Normans recognized the importance of the location, which offered easy access to supplies coming by sea and also guarded the land route through the border region. Rather than erecting an earth-and-timber castle to swiftly take over the site, the Normans decided to construct a more permanent stone castle in 1067. Today, Chepstow's sturdy hall-keep at the centre of the elongated site demands attention. Archaeologists have identified the great rectangular tower as Britain's oldest surviving secular structure.

**ABOVE:** *A lavishly carved Norman archway adorns the original first-floor entrance to the great keep, through which interior arcading is visible. Roman-era tiles are clearly visible in the surrounding walls.*

**ABOVE LEFT:** *Once fronted with a portcullis, a curious late-medieval doorway, fitted with three triangular peep-holes, still guards the entrance into Marten's Tower.*

## A Bastion for a Lord

With elements from every major period of castle building, Chepstow Castle chronicles the impact of the Norman conquest on the Welsh Marches. Its linear layout features three distinct baileys — upper, middle and lower — shrewdly constructed so that each could sustain itself as a 'mini-stronghold' during a siege. The imposing twin-towered gatehouse and immense D-shaped tower still guard the main entrance, which opens into the lower bailey, where Roger Bigod III spearheaded the castle's final phase of construction.

Overlooking the bending river immediately behind the great gatehouse, Bigod's complex hall-block, which is really two buildings in one, embodied medieval affluence. The eastern section quartered garrison officers and allowed direct access to the northern gatetower, which held the prison. Sandwiched between the officers' quarters and the lord's grandiose apartments, the kitchen serviced the needs of castle inhabitants. Bigod's residence featured the great hall, buttery and pantry at first-floor level and a large storage cellar and double-latrines occupied the ground floor. The ornate hall still displays traces of paint and elaborately sculpted windows.

Across the lower bailey, Roger Bigod erected what is now known as Marten's Tower, arguably his most impressive contribution at Chepstow. As a self-contained unit, the heavily defended tower held all the domestic conveniences and security devices residents would require. The tower was later named after Henry Marten (1602–80), one of the signatories of King Charles I's death warrant. The four-storey building featured elegant paintings, windows with seats, fireplaces, latrines and a private chapel. Portcullises barricaded doorways and pyramidal spurs buttressed the tower against undermining.

BELOW: *Commanding sheer-sided cliffs along the River Wye, Chepstow Castle guarded a strategic transit route between England and Wales. From the riverside below, supplies were hauled into the castle and taken directly into the great keep, which controlled the site.*

RIGHT: *Despite the relative simplicity of its exterior walls, the interior of Chepstow's great hall-keep displayed all the grandeur its builders could achieve, including ornately carved corbels, window frames and archways.*

RIGHT: *Once the only landward entry into the medieval town of Chepstow, the well-preserved, battlemented town gate dates to the late 13th century.*

Crowned with its very own stone security force, a set of carved figures, the D-shaped tower presented an impression of power and invincibility.

William Marshal, Earl of Pembroke (*c.* 1146–1219) and one of medieval Wales' greatest castle-builders, also left a lasting legacy at Chepstow. The curtain wall separating the lower and middle baileys sports two of the earl's trademark round towers. After Marshal's death in 1219, his sons enclosed the lower bailey with a curtain wall and added the monumental twin-towered gatehouse. They also heightened the stone keep and added the barbican to safeguard the upper bailey.

## A French Keep

Beyond the middle ward, the great hall-keep towers over the rest of the castle. Begun in 1067 by William FitzOsbern, Earl of Hereford and a

childhood friend of Duke William of Normandy, the building is an outstanding example of a very early, very French design: a stone hall/hall-keep rather than a tower-keep. The massive three-storey rectangle contained a basement and a first-floor hall. The upper floor, added by the Marshals in the 13th century, probably held private apartments. Notable surviving features in the empty shell include sculpted faces, red tiling from the Roman period and joist holes for supporting a timber floor. An ornate Norman archway, which is cut into the eastern façade, pinpoints the first-floor entrance to the keep.

## The Age of Artillery

Although Chepstow escaped devastation during the English Civil War, the castle was re-fortified shortly thereafter. The advent of handguns and heavy artillery prompted the construction of new defensive mechanisms. The entire southern wall was strengthened to withstand the pounding of siege cannons. Towers were plugged with earth and gunports replaced arrow slits. A new fighting platform defended the upper bailey. Although it was garrisoned until 1690, the castle experienced no further military action. Instead, the imposing stronghold fell into ruin. In the 1950s, the building's owner, D.R. Lysaght, transferred the care of the castle to the State.

Now maintained by Cadw, Chepstow Castle continues to challenge archaeologists, who have reconsidered their understanding of the site. Not only did it serve as the powerful fortress of the Marcher Lords of Striguil, but Chepstow Castle also fulfilled a critical ceremonial role, the particulars of which are only just beginning to come to light. The castle is open throughout the year for an entrance fee.

ABOVE: *The castle's defensive power is emphasized with massive round towers, two of which front the main gatehouse. The even larger, spurred Marten's Tower, still crowned with battlements and stone sentinels, plunges into the adjacent ditch. Its most notable 'guest', Henry Marten, occupied the heavily defended yet comfortable tower for 20 years.*

## HISTORY

**1st century AD** – Romans construct fortlet at site.

**1270** – Llywelyn ap Gruffydd destroys castle; Gilbert de Clare II rebuilds.

**1278** – Castle reaches its full extent.

**1314** – Gilbert de Clare III dies at the Battle of Bannockburn; Edward II appoints royal custodians.

**1316** – Llywelyn Bren, Lord of Senghennydd, attacks castle, destroys town and mills.

**1317**– Edward II grants castle to Hugh le Despenser, Eleanor de Clare's husband, who renovates great hall.

**1326** – Despenser and Edward II shelter at castle, where they deposit half the king's treasure.

**1327** – William, Lord Zouche, besieges castle on behalf of Queen Isabella; constable John de Felton forfeits castle after securing safe passage for himself and Hugh, the Despenser heir.

**1328** – The widowed Eleanor de Clare regains rights to castle.

**1329** – Lord Zouche and Eleanor de Clare, now married, unsuccessfully besiege castle.

**1330** – Eleanor de Clare regains castle and lordship of Glamorgan.

**1349** – Castle declared to have no value.

**1416** – Isabel le Despenser passes castle to husband, Richard Beauchamp, Earl of Worcester.

**1422** – Richard Beauchamp, Earl of Warwick, Isabel's second husband, makes repairs.

**1486** – Jasper Tudor acquires the greatly decayed castle.

**1593** – Henry Herbert, Earl of Pembroke, leases castle to Thomas Lewis, who quarries site for building material.

**1640s** – Parliamentarians besiege castle and construct redoubt near hornwork.

**1870s** – John Patrick Crichton Stuart, 3rd Marquess of Bute, begins restoration and documentation programme.

**1928** – John Crichton Stuart, 4th Marquess, begins 11-year restoration project.

# Caerphilly Castle

Intentionally selecting a low-lying spot surrounded on three sides by high hills, Gilbert de Clare II, Lord of Glamorgan and Earl of Gloucester (1243–95), astutely modelled his new Welsh fortress on Kenilworth Castle (see pages 31–3), which he had seen while participating in the siege there in 1266. When finished, de Clare had erected the first completely concentric castle to be built entirely from scratch in Britain and a fortress that was second only to Windsor (see pages 43–5) in size. Ultimately, this 'walls-within-walls' structure became the archetype for other concentric castles, including those built by de Clare's rival, Edward I, in North and Mid Wales (see pages 124–35), which represent the apex of castle-building in Britain.

### Vital Water Defences

Caerphilly's concentric design featured a series of embedded masonry defences, its towers and gatehouses rising progressively taller the closer they were to the centre of the great fortress. Yet, this powerful castle was not just defended with rings of stonework. Just as crucial to the concentric plan were the water defences, which de Clare created by redirecting and damming two streams to encircle the masonry fortifications: Nant y Gledyr and Nant yr Aber. Crossing the water was difficult at best, and impossible without proper preparation, as any attacking force had to ford the lakes to reach each successive gateway and then proceed with their assault.

### Caerphilly's Gatehouses

To gain access to the inner bailey, residents, visitors and besiegers had to cross the two bridges that

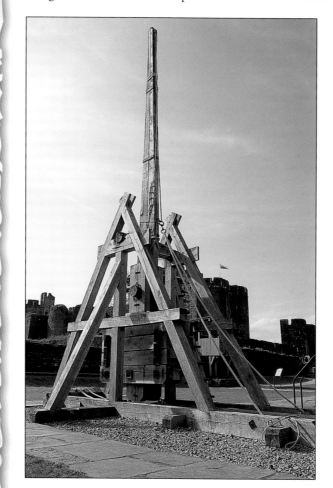

**ABOVE:** *A reconstructed ballista, a giant mechanized crossbow, is poised to strike man and beast with iron-tipped darts.*

**LEFT:** *Worked with springs, powered by a counterweight mechanism and able to hit targets accurately at about 500 yards (460 metres), the trebuchet struck fear into the hearts of the hardiest of soldiers.*

**OPPOSITE:** *Successively taller towers and protective moats spanned by drawbridges accentuate Caerphilly Castle's famed concentric design and stone-and-water defences.*

spanned the water defences and then pass through a series of gatehouses. Dominated by two massive polygonal towers, the outer, eastern gatehouse formed the first barrier. Arrow slits penetrated its walls, while a portcullis and six slender murder holes defended the gate passage and guardrooms flanked each side.

Beyond the outer gatehouse, the southern and northern platforms supported domestic facilities, including the water mill, latrine block, a watergate and a spillway. Two smaller gateways anchored each end. Just past the platforms, another twin-towered gatehouse offered only modest protection from the enemy. Upon breaching this gateway, however, invaders would have found themselves confronted by the gargantuan inner gatehouse and two massive round towers. Today, the south-east tower leans precariously, as it has for centuries, more the victim of subsidence than the battering of siege engines.

The attractive east gatehouse, the first of its kind in Wales and, arguably, Caerphilly's finest structure, dominates the inner bailey. Similar to the great gatehouse at Tonbridge in Kent, which was erected in 1275 by Richard de Clare, Gilbert's father, this powerful building functioned as a keep-gatehouse and could stand on its own during a siege. It also served as the constable's residence and provided entry into the towered, rectangular core of the castle.

### Interior Design

Thick curtain walls and four huge round towers capably defended the inner bailey, which served as a hive of activity throughout the Middle Ages. Modern banners colour the walls of the great hall today, which was largely restored by the marquesses of Bute in the 19th and 20th centuries, and the central fireplace hints at the room's original grandeur. Skilfully carved corbels adorned with three heads still observe

wandering guests, as they did centuries ago. A crowned face may represent Edward II, a close friend of one of the castle's historic owners, Hugh le Despenser (1262–1326), while a lavishly bedecked female figure may depict that notorious king's treacherous wife, Queen Isabella. A bearded face may indicate Despenser himself.

### The People's Fort

Like the eastern gatehouses, those on the west decrease in height from the taller interior gatehouse to the lower outer gateway. They also stand at different levels in relation to each other. It is possible that they were built this way to interfere with any assault. The outermost gatehouse now faces directly into the revetment of the western hornwork. Also known as the western island or Y Weringaer, 'the people's fort', the hornwork may have been the last place of refuge for local townsfolk during a siege.

Though revetted by a low stone wall, the irregularly shaped earthen platform was apparently never completed. Drawbridges linked the hornwork to the inner bailey and to the northern side of the castle. In the 1960s, archaeologists found remnants of the Roman fort across the moat on the opposite side of the hornwork.

Even though its role in Welsh history was relatively short-lived and came late in the annals of British castle-building, Caerphilly Castle remains one of Wales' most important architectural contributions. Accurately restored by the marquesses of Bute, and the moat cautiously re-flooded by the Ministry of Works, who took over the castle in 1950, Caerphilly stands as a monument to the power and wealth of Gilbert de Clare. It also indicates the strength of the threat he felt from Llywelyn ap Gruffydd, the last native Prince of Wales. The quintessential concentric fortress, Caerphilly inspires awe. Cadw opens the castle daily for an entrance fee.

ABOVE: *A series of massive vertical buttresses front the southern dam. At the southernmost end, sluicegates once managed water movement through the main outflow channel, which regulated the height of the southern lake.*

## HISTORY

**1106** – Henry I appoints Roger, Bishop of Salisbury, to administer lordship; construction begins on ringwork castle.

**1136** – Maurice de Londres kills Gwenllian, wife of Gruffydd ap Rhys, during a battle at Maes Gwenllian.

**1139** – De Londres acquires lordship and castle.

**1190** – Rhys ap Gruffydd, the Lord Rhys, repairs castle.

**1215** – Rhys Grug burns castle during Welsh raid on South Wales.

**1231** – Llywelyn ab Iorwerth assaults castle.

**1244** – Payn de Chaworth begins re-fortifying castle with stone.

**1257** – Welsh attack Kidwelly; fire damages town but not castle.

**1361** – Blanche, John of Gaunt's wife, acquires castle as rightful heir.

**1399** – Castle becomes Crown property with accession of Henry IV.

**1403** – Castle endures three-week assault by Welsh supporting Owain Glyndŵr.

**1422** – Construction essentially completed.

**1485** – Henry VII grants castle to Sir Rhys ap Thomas.

**1531** – Upon the execution of owner Rhys ap Gruffydd for treason, ownership of Kidwelly reverts to the monarchy.

**1609** – James I holds court at castle.

**1630** – The Vaughans of Golden Grove, Carmarthenshire, acquire castle.

**Late 18th century** – John Vaughan makes minor repairs.

**1927** – Castle passes into State care.

# Kidwelly Castle

Kidwelly Castle in Carmarthenshire is an anomaly. Perched on the edge of a hillside directly overlooking the River Gwendraeth and a tiny neighbouring village, this massive stronghold startles the senses. The hulking gatehouse looms overhead, at once intimidating and enticing. Originally built as a partial ringwork fortress by Roger, the Norman Bishop of Salisbury, re-fortification in stone transformed a simple stronghold into a powerful D-shaped concentric castle, the only one of its kind in Wales.

### Norman Origins

Forming the rounded face of the castle's 'D' shape, Bishop Roger's semi-circular embankment and ditch buttressed the landward side and provided additional support for the 14th-century curtain wall added by the de Chaworth family. Best

ABOVE: *Linking medieval Kidwelly's town walls with its D-shaped castle, the now ruined gatehouse guards the southern end of Castle Street.*
BELOW: *Kidwelly Castle's massive great gatehouse still intimidates. Towering overhead, the powerful structure possessed all the essential defences a lord needed to ensure his safety.*

viewed from the wall-walk or approached from ground level, the Norman-era earthworks have persevered despite time and the impact of erosion and later building works. They attest to the skills of medieval engineers who began the castle and its associated town walls so long ago.

## Strengthened with Stone

It took a series of assaults by the Welsh to spur owners into strengthening the ringwork with stone. Held by the de Chaworths in the latter part of the 13th and early 14th centuries, the masonry castle emanates an obvious attitude of invulnerability. Its mammoth round towers steadfastly defended the square-shaped core of Kidwelly Castle and also provided living quarters for the lord and his household. Foundations of two halls, a kitchen range, the lord's solar and other structures inside the inner bailey indicate that this was the bustling hub of the castle.

Rising three storeys, the complex gatehouse quartered the porter, the constable and probably other soldiers. It also contained a kitchen, several latrines, a hall, fireplaces and a pit prison, which plunged into the earth from the easternmost gatetower. Equipped with two portcullises, machicolations, murder holes, arrow slits and draw bars, the gate passage allowed only the most powerful enemy into the inner bailey. Everything about the gatehouse, from its bleak grey stonework to the sheer bulk of the twin towers, screams power and intimidation. With the addition of a towered outer curtain wall and imposing gatehouse in the early 14th century, Kidwelly Castle formally came into its own as one of Wales' mightiest concentric fortresses.

Managed by Cadw, Kidwelly Castle is open to visitors daily throughout the year for an entrance fee.

**ABOVE:** *Embedded in the naturally sloping hillside facing the River Gwendraeth, Kidwelly Castle's imposing chapel tower is supported by enormous pyramidal buttresses, which climb well up the side of the massive structure. The angular sacristy rises up its southern side.*

# Pembroke Castle

## HISTORY

1093 – Castle first erected on site.

1096 – Gerald de Windsor, constable of the castle, uses trickery to force Welsh retreat.

1102 – Arnulf de Montgomery forfeits castle.

1138 – Gilbert FitzGilbert de Clare becomes 1st Earl of Pembroke.

1148 – Richard de Clare 'Strongbow' begins stone construction at castle.

1169–70 – Strongbow stages invasion of Ireland from castle.

1405 – Welsh capture constable, Thomas Roche, during Glyndŵr Rebellion.

1413 – Henry V creates his son, Humphrey, as Duke of Gloucester and Earl of Pembroke.

1453 – Henry VI appoints half-brother, Jasper Tudor, as Earl of Pembroke.

1457 – Margaret Beaufort, wife of the late Edmund Tudor, gives birth to a son, named Harri (Henry).

1471 – Jasper flees to France with nephew, Harri Tudor.

1485 – Harri Tudor lands in Pembrokeshire en route to Bosworth field; he regains control of Pembroke Castle, before heading to Bosworth to confront Richard III and become Henry VII; Jasper Tudor regains earldom.

1532 – Queen Anne Boleyn becomes Marchioness of Pembroke.

1648 – Oliver Cromwell slights castle after seven-week siege.

1880s – J.R. Cobb initiates extensive restoration programme.

1930s – Major General Sir Ivor Philipps completes restoration.

In 1081, William the Conqueror travelled across Wales to Pembrokeshire to meet with Rhys ap Tewdwr, King of Deheubarth, but it took the Normans another decade to finally occupy the region. Rhys's death in 1093 caused infighting among his sons, which led to a regional power vacuum. Seizing the moment, the Normans swiftly established themselves at the western end of a steep-sided promontory overlooking the tidal waters of the Pembroke River. There, Arnulf de Montgomery erected an earth-and-timber fortress and commanded the site as Earl of Pembroke. Subsequent holders of the title went on to influence monarchs from what became the mightiest castle in western Wales – powerful Pembroke.

## One of a Kind

Pembroke Castle retained its timber defences until the early 13th century, when William Marshal (*c.* 1146–1219), Regent of England and a signatory of the Magna Carta, became earl. Probably inspired by the designs of castles built by King Philip Augustus in France, Marshal began his masterpiece – the free-standing domed keep – shortly after arriving at the castle in 1204. Ultimately, the Marshal stronghold occupied what became the inner ward. It contained the original Norman hall, the D-shaped horseshoe gate and his pride and joy, the innovative round keep.

Unique not just to Wales but also to the rest of Britain, this great cylinder rises over 80 feet (24.4 metres) high and measures about 52 feet (15.8 metres) across. A spiral staircase climbs within the thickness of the walls from ground level to the rooftop, where panoramic views of the town and surrounding countryside may be enjoyed. Notable features include the 13-foot (4-metre) thick walls, fireplaces on the first and second floors, an ornate window with seats on the second storey, putlog holes for timber hoarding and arrow slits. Curiously, the keep lacked any sanitary facilities.

## Original Feature

Beyond Marshal's great keep at the north-eastern corner of the inner bailey, Pembroke Castle's most intriguing feature – an enormous natural cavern called the 'wogan' – hides underground. It can only be reached via a steep staircase that spirals into the bowels of the earth. This dripping hole once allowed sailing ships to safely unload supplies beneath the castle. Today, the river has receded well away

OPPOSITE: *William Marshal's great keep dominates the inner bailey at Pembroke Castle.*

LEFT: *Once washing the castle's foundations, the rapidly shifting tidal waters of the River Pembroke formed a natural moat and also allowed shipping traffic to sail into the 'wogan'.*

BELOW: *The Norman Old Hall is one of the castle's earliest stone structures. It held a ground-level basement and a first-floor hall, lit by a large window that overlooked the inner bailey.*

ABOVE: *Pembroke's mammoth gatehouse contained both heavy defences and comfortable, at least by the standards of the times, living quarters. Tradition has it that Henry VII was born in the neighbouring tower that bears his name, but more than likely the gatehouse witnessed the historic birth.*

from the mouth of the wogan, so visitors can explore the cavern from inside or peer into it from the pathway that circles the castle.

### Further Improvements

In 1247, the earldom of Pembroke and the castle passed through the Marshal female line from Joan de Muchensey to her husband, William de Valence. De Valence erected the castle's great gatehouse and outer defences, which enclosed not only the fortress, but the town of Pembroke as well. One of Britain's first keep-gatehouses, the well-defended structure contained arrow slits, two portcullises, sets of heavy timber doors secured in place by iron draw bars and three murder holes to frustrate an enemy attack. The upper storeys held comfortable living quarters.

Riddled with mural passages and a lengthy wall-walk, Pembroke Castle's curtain wall is pierced by several round towers, a rectangular bastion and two watergates. The tower just west

of the great gatehouse is known as the Henry VII Tower, as it has a reputation as the king's birth-place. However, many scholars believe that Margaret Beaufort (1443–1509) would have had more comfort giving birth to the future king in one of the upper chambers in the gatehouse.

### Restoration

In the 19th century, the antiquarian J.R. Cobb began to restore the crumbling castle that had dutifully served the Earls of Pembroke and the Tudor Dynasty for so long. Continuing Cobb's efforts, Major General Sir Ivor Philipps completed a full-scale restoration project, which largely returned this great fortress to its pre-Civil War condition. Today, Pembroke Castle is managed by the Pembroke Castle Trust, and is open for an entrance fee through-out the year. Lengthy portions of the original town walls still enclose much of Pembroke town. Highlights include Barnard's Tower, the Gun Tower and remnants of the Westgate.

# Harlech Castle

Perhaps more than any other castle, majestic Harlech highlights the successes and failures of the Welsh during their long struggle for independence from the English. Erected as part of Edward I's grand plan of subjugation, the castle stands in Gwynedd as an omnipresent monument to the engineering genius of the king's master of works, James of St George (c. 1230–1309), who served as castle constable for the final three years of construction. The stronghold is also an ever-present reminder of Edward's obsession with conquering Wales. Commanding a rocky hump known as Harlech Dome, the brawny castle combined nature's gifts with innovative defences to present an air of impregnability that was intended to suppress further rebellion. In reality, what Harlech exuded was the illusion of impregnability, which the Welsh repeatedly challenged.

## The Way from the Sea

Dominated by what is probably Britain's most impressive great gatehouse, Harlech Castle displays concentric design in all its glory. Its outer defences rising from rocky outcrops, Harlech Castle seems more like

ABOVE: *Harlech's great gatehouse exudes an air of domestic comfort. Staircases and accommodation once filled the towers.*

BELOW: *A 19-foot (5.8-metre) high turret adds height to the round north-west tower, which rose almost 50 feet (15.2 metres) to guard the 'way from the sea'.*

## HISTORY

1283 – Edward I begins castle at Harlech.

1289 – Construction completed at a cost of £9,000.

1290 – Master James of St George becomes constable.

1294 – Madog ap Llywelyn leads Welsh assault against castle.

1295 – Castle defences strengthened.

1323 – Headquarters for royalist forces led by Sir Gruffydd Llwyd, Sheriff of Merioneth.

1404 – Harlech becomes Owain Glyndŵr's main residence and a meeting place for the Welsh parliament.

1408 – English army captures castle, destroys outer wall during siege.

1468 – Garrisoned for Lancastrians during Wars of the Roses; constable Dafydd ab Ieuan ab Einion shelters Queen Margaret of Anjou, but surrenders after Yorkist siege.

1564 – Castle described as a ruin.

1604 – Merioneth Assizes.

1647 – Parliamentarian forces led by Major-General Mytton slight castle.

1914 – Office of Works takes over responsibility for castle.

1918 – Consolidation begins.

1969 – Care passes to Secretary of State for Wales.

1986 – UNESCO designates Harlech Castle as a World Heritage Site.

**ABOVE:** *Also known as 'Weathercock Tower' and 'Bronwen Tower', the south-western tower opened at ground level to the kitchen block, now little more than foundations, which serviced the adjoining great hall. The tower also afforded views to the sea.*

one of Snowdonia's peaks than a man-made fortress. The proximity of the sea, which once washed the base of Harlech Dome but has long since retreated, provided Edward with the ideal site for a castle. Even today, ascending the legendary 'way from the sea', its 127 steps climbing some 200 feet (61 metres) from road level to the outer ward, causes the fittest of visitors to pause, catch their breath and fully appreciate the impact such a laborious journey would have had on an enemy force.

### The Architecture of Power

At Harlech, geology dictated the cramped but strategically efficient layout of the castle, which Master James manipulated to great effect.

Fronted on two sides by a deep rock-cut ditch, the low outer wall traced the perimeter of the inner defences. Its lower corner bastions and turreted outer gateway provided a first line of defence against an assault and limited access to the narrow outer bailey. Immediately inside, the twin-towered gatehouse acted as a giant barrier to any forward movement, while massive round towers possessed the four corners of the inner wall.

For its builders, Harlech Castle was an exercise in creating symmetry and power. Their greatest achievement, the three-storey main gate-house, still dwarfs anyone bold enough to make an approach. The gate passage featured three sets of heavy timber doors, three portcullises,

arrow slits that allowed soldiers in the adjoining guardrooms to shoot at intruders and murder holes overhead. Well-appointed residential suites filled the upper storeys, bedchambers and latrines were in the main towers and a chapel was situated in the gap between them. Meanwhile, there was a great chamber or hall on the southern side and a smaller private chamber on the north. Leading directly to the first-floor apartments, which probably housed the constable, an unusual staircase allowed movement between the gatehouse and the rest of the castle, even when the gate passage was secured.

## Man of Harlech

Ironically, Harlech's façade of invulnerability was breached on more than one occasion, most notably when Owain Glyndŵr (c. 1354–1416) seized the castle in 1404 and held onto it for four years. Edward I might have blanched at the thought that, only a century after his death, a self-proclaimed native 'Prince of Wales' had captured the powerful fortress and made it his Welsh headquarters.

Each step around Harlech Castle gives visitors not just a real sense of the power of the concentric design, but also offers superb views towards Snowdonia. On clear days, even Criccieth Castle is visible to the north-west. Managed by Cadw, Harlech remains one of Wales' finest treasures, and is open daily throughout the year for an entrance fee.

ABOVE: *Combining structural power, a concentric design and expansive views to Snowdonia and the Llŷn Peninsula, the builders of Harlech Castle intended it to be completely invincible. In the end, the Welsh broke through the defences.*

## HISTORY

1173 – Llywelyn ab Iorwerth, Prince of Gwynedd, is born at Tomen Castell.

Early 13th century – Llywelyn begins stone castle on ridgetop north of motte.

1240 – The death of Llywelyn ab Iorwerth leads to revolt among Welsh princes of Gwynedd.

1255 – Llywelyn ap Gruffydd, the elder Llywelyn's grandson, gains power over all of Gwynedd.

1267 – English King Henry III signs the Treaty of Montgomery, officially recognizing Llywelyn ap Gruffydd as the Prince of Wales in exchange for the Welshman's sworn fealty.

1282 – Llywelyn ap Gruffydd, the first and last native Prince of Wales, dies during a skirmish with English soldiers at Cilmeri near Builth Wells.

1283 – Edward I's army captures castle from the Welsh.

1290 – English withdraw from castle.

1402 – Owain Glyndŵr imprisons Lord Grey of Ruthin at castle.

Late 15th century – Maredudd ab Ieuan leases site and heightens keep.

1848 – Lord Willoughby de Eresby begins restoration.

1930 – Mrs C. Williams of Bryn Tirion places castle in State care.

# Dolwyddelan Castle

Even though native kings and princes commanded the countryside long before the Normans arrived in Wales, the Welsh felt little need to construct castles on a scale even close to the size and strength of those built by the outsiders who had systematically seized so much of their homeland. Consequently, in a land known for its castles, surprisingly few were built by the Welsh themselves. Most Welsh-built castles hide in the desolate, windswept mountainous areas of Mid Wales and North Wales, where *Cymraeg*, the native language, still resonates in village shops, schools and chapels.

### Princes of Gwynedd

Among Welsh castle-builders, Llywelyn ab Iorwerth and his grandson, Llywelyn ap Gruffydd, princes of Gwynedd in the 13th century, left arguably the greatest legacy to their countrymen and -women. Better known as Llywelyn the Great, the elder Llywelyn erected several substantial stone castles, including Castell y Bere in Mid Wales and Castell Carndochan, Dolbadarn and Ewloe castles in North Wales.

The younger Llywelyn, the first and last native Prince of Wales, strengthened Ewloe and contributed Dolforwyn Castle in Mid Wales. Of the Welsh-built strongholds in Gwynedd, both Llywelyns are associated with the compact but immensely evocative stone-enclosure castle at Dolwyddelan.

### Mountain Castle

Strategically built to command two communications routes across Snowdonia,

ABOVE: *The heart of Dolwyddelan Castle is its simple rectangular keep, probably begun by Llywelyn the Great in the early 13th century.*

BELOW: *Dolwyddelan's rocky surroundings blend with the masonry castle to form an intimidating vision of strength and durability in the rugged landscape.*

Dolwyddelan Castle dominates its rocky surroundings, the foreboding brown-grey stonework mirroring the intimidating mountains that engulf the region. Although cited by many historians as Llywelyn ab Iorwerth's birthplace, the Welsh prince himself probably built the masonry castle early in the 13th century. Llywelyn's stronghold featured a single rectangular keep, which was accessed by a forebuilding, enclosed by a stone curtain wall and a simple gateway, and defended on two sides by a deep ditch. Restored in the 19th century, the stone keep originally rose over two levels and contained the basement, which was only accessible through a trap-door in the ceiling, and the first-floor great chamber, which was equipped with a fireplace and a latrine.

Across the inner ward from the keep, the ruined West Tower barely endures the passage of time. Possibly built by Llywelyn ap Gruffydd or his nemesis, Edward I, after he seized the castle in 1283, the rectangular tower offered additional residential space, including latrines. The large first-floor fireplace implies the presence of a great hall, which may have been much grander than the one inside the keep.

## Tomen Castell

Arguably of greater interest is the tree-covered hill adjacent to farm buildings directly across the A470. Llywelyn's father, Iorwerth, or an earlier ancestor, probably modified the hillock into a substantial motte castle in the early 12th century. Known as Tomen Castell, the surprisingly huge motte more than likely served as the birthplace of Llywelyn the Great – one of Wales' greatest heroes – in 1173. Like its more formidable neighbour across the road, the humble earth-and-timber castle deserves recognition for the key role it played in Welsh history.

The strenuous trek up to the masonry castle gives modern visitors a feel for the strategic value of the location, which was never taken by siege.

Dolwyddelan Castle offers stunning views of Snowdonia's craggy landscape and the neighbouring fields still harbouring Tomen Castell. Maintained by Cadw, the castle is open throughout the year, for an entrance fee. The entrance to the historic site itself is after a cluster of farm buildings.

**ABOVE:** *Heavily restored in the 19th century, Dolwyddelan Castle's rectangular keep offers palpable stability to the otherwise ruinous site, which includes the crumbling West Tower. Ideally situated on a steep-sloped rocky crag, the Welsh-built castle remains one of the finest examples of its kind.*

## HISTORY

AD 77 – Romans establish fort at Segontium.

1090 – Hugh d'Avranches, Earl of Chester, begins motte castle.

1115 – Welsh princes recover control of Caernarfon.

1283 – Edward I begins castle, directed by Master James of St George.

1284 – Queen Eleanor gives birth to Edward of Caernarfon.

1285 – Town walls substantially complete.

1286 – Sir Otto de Grandison, justiciar of North Wales, becomes constable.

1294 – Welsh rebellion led by Madog ap Llywelyn causes heavy damage to town walls.

1295 – English repair castle and town walls.

1301 – Edward of Caernarfon becomes first English Prince of Wales.

1330 – Work on castle stops at a total cost of £25,000; King's and Queen's Gates remain unfinished.

1399 – Richard II takes refuge at castle.

1401 – Owain Glyndŵr attacks castle, Welsh suffer 300 casualties.

1646 – Royalist constable John Lord Byron surrenders castle to General Mytton; castle begins to decay.

1660 – Parliament orders destruction of castle and town walls.

Late 19th century – Sir Llywelyn Turner, deputy constable, directs renovation.

1894 – Prince and Princess of Wales visit castle during National Eisteddfod.

1907 – Edward VII visits castle.

1908 – Responsibility for castle passes to Office of Works.

1911 – Future Prime Minister David Lloyd George, castle constable, oversees formal investiture of George V's eldest son, Albert Edward, as Prince of Wales.

1969 – Lord Snowdon, castle constable, oversees formal investiture of Elizabeth II's eldest son, Charles, as Prince of Wales.

1986 – UNESCO designates castle and town walls as a World Heritage Site.

# Caernarfon Castle

That Caernarfon Castle so closely resembles the walls of mighty Constantinople is no mere coincidence. Nor is the notion that Edward I envisioned himself as great a king as the Byzantine emperors. After the English king completed his second campaign against the Welsh, whom he felt he had finally conquered in 1283, he believed his achievements were comparable to Emperor Constantine's. And the omens seemed to support his belief. Not only had Caernarfon served as a Roman outpost during Constantine's reign, but when Edward prepared to establish his new castle, reports widely circulated that a tomb belonging to the Roman emperor himself had been discovered in Caernarfon. Certain his destiny paralleled that of the Roman emperors, Edward ordered his castle to be built on the shores of the River Seiont, close to the ageing Roman fort, and designed it to model the walls of Constantinople.

### An Imperial Seat

Commanding a triangular chunk of land surrounded on three sides by the waters of the River Seiont, the Cadnant brook and the Menai Strait, Caernarfon Castle and its circuit of medieval walls embodied Edward's vision of himself as a warrior-king who stood head and shoulders above the common man. Unlike his other great fortresses in North Wales, the imperial stronghold at Caernarfon featured giant polygonal towers crowned with battlements, the walls banded with stone of contrasting colour. Certainly, anyone approaching the castle would appreciate its singular importance as a king's palace and fortress.

In many respects, Caernarfon resembles the hourglass-shaped Conwy Castle (see pages 130–32), which Edward had begun a few months earlier. Unlike Conwy, however, Caernarfon Castle featured two prominent gatehouses. The King's Gate, the main entrance, looked into the town as it does today, while the Queen's Gate watched over the waters of the Cadnant at the north-eastern corner of the site, where traces of the original motte survive. Even though workers never completed either gatehouse, the structures had the strength to withstand the most determined of assaults.

### Distinct Enclosures

Caernarfon Castle consists of two distinct areas that are enclosed by powerful towered walls. Had the fortress been completed, a cross-wall would probably have provided a physical barrier between the two sections. The royal apartments, situated in heavily defended towers, and the domestic facilities, including the great hall and kitchen range, occupied the lower-lying bailey to the west. The basement entrance into the unusual well tower allowed supplies brought by ship to be carried directly into the castle, and a lead-lined 50-foot (15-metre) deep cistern provided ground level access to the castle's water supply.

ABOVE: *A finely carved but weather-worn statue of King Edward II overlooks the King's Gate, the main entrance to his birthplace.*

OPPOSITE: *Edward I's official residence at Caernarfon, the battlemented Eagle Tower, displays the king's fanciful connection to the Emperor Constantine.*

**ABOVE:** *Majestic Caernarfon Castle emanates grandeur and power, qualities Edward I believed he possessed. His stronghold in north-western Wales remains testimony not just to the king's personal sense of worth but also reflects the intensity with which he dreaded further revolts from the Welsh.*

**OPPOSITE ABOVE:** *Twin polygonal towers defend the main entrance. Known as the King's Gate, the structure was never fully completed. Even so, the gateway managed to both intimidate and welcome.*

### Caernarfon's Towers

Of the castle's four-storey, turreted towers, the Eagle Tower is Caernarfon's grandest. Adorned with stone eagles to symbolize Edward's supposed link to Imperial Rome, this tower commands the westernmost side of the bailey and served as the king's quarters. Besides offering private access to the sea, the lavishly equipped tower contained residential chambers, an octagonal chapel, an ornate fireplace and the essential latrine. Historians speculate that the Eagle Tower probably served as Prince Edward's birthplace in 1284.

The castle's other towers resembled the Eagle Tower in plan, if not in purpose. Between the Black Tower and the Queen's Gate on the upper bailey, the Cistern Tower retains the stone-lined tank that gathered rainwater. Today, the towers house exhibits that relate the history of the castle and the Princes of Wales, and the Queen's Tower now serves as the home for the Regimental Museum of the Royal Welch Fusiliers. Interestingly, neither the Cistern Tower nor the Black Tower possess doorways into the bailey at ground level. The presence of the earthen motte, which was levelled in the late 19th century, probably precluded their use.

Beyond the north-east tower, the 800-yard (730-metre) long town walls begin their D-shaped loop round medieval Caernarfon. Defended with eight rounded towers and two twin-towered gatehouses, the battlemented walls survive in fine condition. For a time, the renovated East Gate served as the town hall and later as the guildhall. The West Gate, also known as the Porth yr Aur, or Golden Gate, still faces the sea.

Caernarfon Castle vigorously showcased Edward I's self-importance, his authoritative power over the Welsh and, in the body of his son, Edward, Prince of Wales, his appropriation of the Welsh crown. Today, the castle not only remains a masterpiece of engineering genius and a monument to the king who built it, but it also stands as an enduring testament to the native Welsh who fought against the English to remain free. The strength of its walls is proportional to the strength of the Welsh spirit.

Cadw opens Caernarfon Castle for a fee throughout the year.

RIGHT: *Positioned immediately alongside the vital well tower, the ruined kitchen block retains fragments of the emplacements for two cooking cauldrons and a drain, which moved water from the tanks serving the adjoining tower.*

## HISTORY

1283 – Edward I designates Llanfaes as Anglesey's seat of government.

1294 – Madog ap Llywelyn leads Welsh revolt.

1295 – Edward I moves population of Llanfaes to Newborough; begins castle and town of Beaumaris.

1331 – Major construction ceases.

1389 – Garrisoned with 20 men in anticipation of a Welsh revolt.

1403 – Welsh capture castle during Owain Glyndŵr's rebellion.

1405 – English retake castle with support from Ireland.

1534 – Castle recorded as a ruin.

1593 – Prisoner and Catholic cleric, Father William Davies, conducts mass in chapel and is later executed.

1642 – Beaumaris is garrisoned for Charles I.

1646 and 1648 – Royalist commander, Colonel Richard Bulkeley, surrenders castle to parliamentarian leader, Major-General Thomas Mytton.

1660 – Castle partly dismantled.

1807 – Thomas James Warren-Bulkeley acquires castle.

1832 – Royal Eisteddfod held at Beaumaris.

1925 – Sir Richard Williams-Bulkeley places castle in State care; consolidation begins.

1986 – UNESCO designates castle as a World Heritage Site.

# Beaumaris Castle

Begun in response to a Welsh revolt in 1294, Anglesey's mighty Beaumaris Castle represents the epitome of Edward I's programme of castle construction in North Wales. Projecting the power and impregnability of English domination, the castle on the fair marsh – *beau mareys* in Anglo-Norman – was strategically located at sea level for easy access to shipping. Indeed, one of its most unusual features, the tidal dock, provided ample mooring space for 40-tonne ships to unload supplies and reinforcements directly into the castle. Today, the sea has retreated from Beaumaris, but the shining waters of its broad moat reflect the past, when the tides ebbed and flowed and safeguarded the mighty castle.

## No Expense Spared

During the first few years of construction, Edward I spent over £7,000 building his perfect concentric castle. His master engineer, James of St George, directed the work of almost 3,000 labourers, who hauled in tonnes of stone, timber, charcoal, lead and tools to tackle the project. The pace of the building effort slowed to a standstill in about 1300, but construction began afresh

after constable John de Metfield complained of defensive weaknesses in 1306. Building continued apace until about 1331, when funds ran out and the monarch's attention shifted to other priorities. Never rising to its full height, the castle seems squat and low-lying. Nonetheless, Beaumaris fully deserves its reputation as the concentric castle par excellence, its complex design completely geared towards repulsing the Welsh, should they dare to attack again.

## Impregnable Walls

Completely enclosed by the moat, the heavily defended castle consisted of two towered walls, one embedded within the other and positioned so that defenders on the inner wall could fire at attackers without striking comrades on the outer wall. The attractive outer wall featured 16 round towers, two simple gateways and the tidal dock. Should an enemy manage to breach the outer walls, the hulking inner walls would confine them in a narrow, now grass-filled, killing ground.

The 15-foot (4.6-metre) thick quadrangular inner curtain wall was defended at each corner with four massive round towers, D-shaped towers planted midway along the east and west

walls and two immense twin-towered gate-houses fronting the north and south sides. One of the wall's more peculiar, albeit innovative, features was a series of back-to-back latrine units. The units had individual doors for privacy, wooden seats for convenience and were fitted with ventilation shafts rising from basement-level pits, which allowed air to circulate and also opened into channels underneath the outer bailey. Accessed periodically along the wall-walk, the latrines offered considerable comfort in an otherwise stark environment.

Truly one of Wales' greatest national treasures, majestic Beaumaris Castle radiates scenic beauty despite its intended role as a subjugator of the Welsh. Swans grace the waters of the moat, making their nests near the angular remains of Llanfaes Gate. Projecting eastward from the castle, the town of Beaumaris retains its medieval character, not only in its layout, but also in historic buildings, such as the Tudor Rose medieval hall-house and Ye Olde Bulls Head Inn.

Beaumaris Castle is managed by Cadw and is open daily throughout the year for an entrance fee.

**ABOVE:** *Although never raised to their full extent, the staggered heights of the round curtain towers positioned along both the inner and outer walls reveal the concentric design employed by Edward I at Beaumaris.*

**OPPOSITE ABOVE:** *The charming chapel royal at Beaumaris survives on the first storey of the Chapel Tower. In their heyday, the now-white walls boasted brilliant colours. The decorative arches allowed passage into the adjoining vestibule and other chambers.*

**OPPOSITE BELOW:** *Once washed by the waters of Conwy Bay, the main entrance to Beaumaris Castle was also known as 'the gate next the sea'. Immediately across the bridge, the castle connected physically to the medieval town walls.*

# Conwy Castle

## HISTORY

1283 – Edward I moves Cistercian abbey from Conwy to Maenan to make space for castle.

1287 – Castle substantially complete.

1292 – Total cost of construction at £15,000.

1294–5 – Edward I resides at castle for six months.

1321 & 1332 – Reports document necessary repairs.

1346 – Major rebuilding effort.

1399 – Richard II receives Henry Percy's assurances of safe passage in chapel royal shortly before his capture and imprisonment at Flint Castle.

1627 – Edward, Lord Conway of Ragley, Charles I's Secretary of State, purchases the decayed castle for £100.

1645 – John Williams, Archbishop of York, re-fortifies castle on behalf of king; shifts allegiance to Parliament to save the town, then under siege by Major-General Mytton.

1646 – Garrison surrenders; parliamentarian governor, Colonel John Carter, initiates repairs.

1655 – Slighting breaches Bakehouse Tower.

1660 – 3rd Lord Conway regains possession of castle.

1665 – Lord Conway dismantles castle and sells lead.

1826 – Construction of Thomas Telford's suspension road bridge.

1848 – Robert Stephenson's tubular railway bridge opens.

1865 – The Hollands, castle tenants, give lease rights to Conwy town officials.

1885 – Queen Victoria designates town mayor as castle constable in perpetuity.

In March of 1283, shortly after seizing the Welsh castle at Dolwyddelan (see pages 122–3), Edward I instigated his second castle-building campaign in Wales. The English king chose to locate the stronghold that became his greatest fortress on a rocky spur in the north of the country that projected outwards into the watery junction between the River Conwy and the Gyffin Stream. Its ultimate form was dictated as much by the lay of the land as by the king's ego and his defensive requirements – Conwy was a royal castle in every sense of the word. It successfully combined architectural grandeur, physical intimidation and palatial accommodation. Bolstered by the ingenuity of his master mason, James of St George, Edward I can rightly be considered to be Britain's greatest castle-building king.

### Double Strength

Conwy Castle seems to rise directly out of the bedrock at its base, creating the impression of complete invulnerability. The linear castle actually consists of two connected strongholds, each dominated by four massive round towers and fronted with narrow barbicans. Though designed to support each other, each side could stand on its own during a siege. The larger, western side of the castle not only overlooked the town and defended against landward invasion, it also provided an impressive array of domestic buildings, including the constable's quarters, accommodation for the garrison, a kitchen tower and the great hall.

A small gateway, reached by passing alongside the enormous 91-foot (27.7-metre) deep, spring-fed well and crossing a bridge, leads into the inner bailey, which housed the royal chambers. Like its counterpart to the west of the cross-wall, the compact royal residence featured an array of domestic units, albeit on a nobler scale. The simple act of walking from the outer bailey into the royal palace visually

OPPOSITE ABOVE: *Though only a shell, the magnificence of Conwy's great hall is best viewed from the battlements. Beyond the farthest tower, the expansive medieval walls entirely enclose the historic town.*

OPPOSITE BELOW: *Plummeting through the bedrock, the deep well still flows with water. Originally, the forbidding structure was lined with stone and capped with a roof.*

BELOW: *Although altered over time with the addition of castellated road and railway bridges, the approach from the River Conwy remains one of the castle's strongpoints.*

ABOVE: *Emerging from their bedrock base, the battlemented King's Tower and Chapel Tower and the towered barbican before them keep watch over the walled town to which they are forever linked.*

1401, Gwilym ap Tudur took the castle by stealth, making his move while all but two members of the garrison prayed in the nearby Church of St Mary and All Saints. The Welsh occupied the castle for two months before the English regained possession.

## Fortified Town

Conwy's complex town walls provided the ideal complement to the hulking castle. Constructed to completely enclose the town, the triangular walls also safeguarded the western side of Edward's castle. They averaged 5½ feet (1.7 metres) in thickness and rose almost 30 feet (9 metres) high. The towers stood another 20 feet (6 metres) above the walls. Today, they survive to their full extent. When considered with the castle, they comprise the finest and best-preserved example of a castle-and-town-wall complex in Britain – and, arguably, in Europe as well. Intended from the outset to accompany the castle, labourers completed both projects within five years, a remarkable achievement.

The town circuit featured three twin-towered gateways and 21 round towers deliberately placed at 50-yard (45-metre) intervals and linked by a continuous wall-walk fitted with removable timber bridges. In the event of an attack, defenders could remove boards running across the rear of each open-backed tower and effectively isolate that tower and the adjoining length of wall. Not only did the inventive design impede enemy progress, it also gave defenders a safety zone from which to fire at attackers.

reinforced the status gap and functional differences between the two sides of the castle.

## The Welsh Fight Back

The Welsh remained unimpressed by Edward I's seemingly impregnable castles in North Wales. In late 1294, they rebelled. By then, Conwy Castle stood almost complete, which must have provided solace in January of 1295, when Madog ap Llywelyn assaulted the site. Ironically, Edward, England's mighty warrior-king, was in residence, and became a prisoner in his own fortress. Food and water supplies dwindled until reinforcements finally arrived from Ireland and forced the Welsh to retreat.

Only during Owain Glyndŵr's 15th-century rebellion did Conwy Castle fall to an enemy. In

Together with Edward's castles at Caernarfon, Harlech and Beaumaris, the powerful castle and medieval town walls at Conwy justifiably deserve their combined designation by UNESCO as a World Heritage Site. The monumental building works at Conwy showcase the engineering genius of their designer, Master James of St George, who fulfilled the English king's demands for a network of castles that displayed his control of the Welsh. Cadw opens Conwy Castle throughout the year for a fee. The town walls are freely accessible.

# Rhuddlan Castle

In 1284, Edward I made law the Statute of Rhuddlan, which forever merged Wales with England. To placate the Welsh nobility who resisted the enforced union, the English king solidified his hold over the Celtic nation by proclaiming his infant son as Prince of Wales: English by blood but Welsh by birthplace and spoken language. The exact location for the king's historic announcement is disputed, but Edward's stronghold at Rhuddlan in Denbighshire – the first of his great concentric fortresses – would have proved an ideal venue for an event of such consequence.

## A Norman Neighbour

In 1277, Edward I mistakenly believed he had conquered the Welsh and effectively ended the rule of their native princes. Establishing new fortresses in North and Mid Wales, he began the initial phase of what became an oppressive ring of castles to rein in the Welsh. Choosing a riverside location, which had earlier been settled by the Saxons and then by the Normans, Edward began a diamond-shaped concentric castle at Rhuddlan. The symbolism of its position was not lost on the king. Rhuddlan's stronger, stone fortress was

BELOW: *Now little more than a shell, the interior of the western gatehouse only hints at the grandeur of its twin-towered façade.*

ABOVE: *Rhuddlan Castle's formidable round towers remain its most impressive feature. Upper levels of the west gatehouse held the castle's main accommodation.*

## HISTORY

AD 921 – Edward the Elder establishes Saxon settlement 'at the mouth of the River Clwyd'.

1063 – Harold Godwinson destroys Gruffydd ap Llywelyn's headquarters at Rhuddlan.

1073 – Robert of Rhuddlan builds Twthill and establishes a small borough, mint and church.

1157–1263 – Control of castle vacillates between English monarchy and Welsh princes.

1240s - Castle still had timber defences and buildings, which historical records document as being repaired at this time.

1277 – Edward I begins construction on stone castle, his second fortress in Wales, a month after starting Flint Castle.

1278 – Edward I and his queen, Eleanor, stay at castle for a week; expansion of medieval town begins.

1280s – Major building programme results in construction of private apartments and a chapel for Queen Eleanor.

1282 – Queen Eleanor gives birth to a daughter, Elizabeth, at the stone castle.

1310 – Historical documents record the existence of 'Bircloyt', a Saxon burh.

14th century – Medieval bridge spanning River Clwyd is rebuilt or repaired on several occasions.

1400 – Owain Glyndŵr devastates Rhuddlan town, but does not take castle.

1944 – Admiral Rowley-Conwy donates castle and surrounding estates to Ministry of Works.

the Norman castle stands fast, a classic motte and bailey. Possibly built over the site of Gruffydd ap Llywelyn's palace, the motte castle commands panoramic views of the River Clwyd and the landscape beyond. Medieval watchmen posted on the summit would have identified an approaching friend or foe easily.

## Edward's Stone Fortress

Relying upon the talents of Master Bertram and Master James of St George, the king inaugurated the first phase of his monumental castle-building programme. Fitted with enormous round corner towers and identical gatehouses, which guarded the western and eastern approaches, Rhuddlan's masonry fortress took over five years and cost £10,000 to complete. Recently consolidated to prevent further decay, the four-storey, twin-towered western gatehouse is the castle's most distinguishing feature. Edward's only other diamond-shaped castle, at Aberystwyth, also dates to 1277, and its ruins still watch the waters of Cardigan Bay as they batter the shoreline.

At Rhuddlan, to provide ships with direct access to the castle, Edward re-routed the course of the River Clwyd for a distance of 2 to 3 miles (3.2 to 4.8km). Employing as many as 66 ditchers digging six days a week, the back-breaking task took three years to complete. The construction of the Dock Gate at the south-west corner of the outer ward allowed ships to moor safely in the shadow of Gillot's Tower.

## Ravaged Rhuddlan

Having supported the royalist cause during the Civil War, the garrison at Rhuddlan finally surrendered to parliamentarian forces in 1646. Two years later, Cromwell's men slighted the

built a few hundred feet north of the primitive motte and bailey, Twthill, which was erected shortly after William I conquered the Saxons in 1066. Deliberately placed almost side-by-side to overlook the River Clwyd, the two castles vividly demonstrated the changes wrought by the Plantagenet kings.

Almost a thousand years after its construction, Twthill seems to persevere by sheer determination. Pummelling rains and natural erosion have degraded the earthen mound and modern buildings encroach upon the bailey, but

stronghold. Townsfolk promptly used the site as a quarry for building material, tearing away the lower courses of stone for private use elsewhere in the town. Nevertheless, Rhuddlan's two castles have steadfastly endured the ravages of time and human consumption. Side by side, they represent the innovations in castle construction that so dramatically impacted the development of Britain's historic landscape.

Cadw opens Rhuddlan Castle for a fee throughout the year. Twthill is freely accessible by making just a short trek to the south-east.

**ABOVE:** *Intentionally diverting the River Clwyd to act as a natural moat and to allow the arrival of supplies and reinforcements by sea, Edward I ordered the construction of a concentric castle at Rhuddlan, which replaced the earlier motte castle, Twthill. Rectangular Gillot's Tower protected the castle dock, where ships moored at high tide.*

**OPPOSITE:** *Rhuddlan's innovative concentric design included a stone revetted moat, which enclosed the portions of the castle where the River Clwyd did not reach. A massive corner tower not only guarded the south-western approach to the castle, it also contained spacious accommodation.*

# GREAT CASTLES OF IRELAND

Centuries before the Normans stormed the island, Gaelic kings commanded Ireland. Internal strife between dynastic families was commonplace. Recognizing an opportunity among the chaos, Henry II encouraged his lords to march into Ireland in 1169. Led by Richard de Clare, who was known as 'Strongbow', the Norman invasion led to dramatic changes not only in social structure, but also in the landscape. To establish themselves swiftly as the land's new overlords, the Normans erected scores of earth-and-timber castles. Many, like the ringwork castles at Limerick and Trim, developed into powerful stone castles. Some, such as Carrickfergus, were conceived as stone castles and retain their intimidating medieval façades. Others, like Kilkenny, grandly served their noble residents until the 20th century. Ireland's classic tower houses, such as the bulking Bunratty, proudly display their medieval trappings, while the ruins at Cashel exude a more otherworldly air. Today, each castle portrays a different, yet equally vital, picture of Ireland's stormy past and, together, they chronicle a history of passion, devotion and startling endurance.

DONEGAL
LONDONDERRY
ANTRIM
CARRICKFERGUS CASTLE
TYRONE
FERMANAGH
ARMAGH
DOWN
SLIGO
MONAGHAN
MAYO
LEITRIM
CAVAN
ROSCOMMON
LOUTH
ROSCOMMON CASTLE
LONGFORD
MEATH
GALWAY
WESTMEATH
TRIM CASTLE
OFFALY
DUBLIN
KILDARE
CLARE
LAOIS
WICKLOW
BUNRATTY CASTLE
KILKENNY CASTLE
CARLOW
LIMERICK CASTLE
TIPPERARY
LIMERICK
KILKENNY
ROCK OF CASHEL
CAHIR CASTLE
WEXFORD
KERRY
WATERFORD
CORK

## HISTORY

1177 – John de Courcy begins castle.

1204 – Hugh de Lacy, Earl of Ulster, evicts de Courcy.

1210 – King John seizes castle; de Lacy flees to France.

1227 – De Lacy regains control of castle and begins new construction.

1264 – William de Burgh acquires earldom of Ulster and castle.

1316 – Edward Bruce captures castle after a year-long siege.

1318 – English regain castle.

1333 – Castle reverts to Crown upon collapse of earldom.

1560 – Defences upgraded for artillery.

1575 –- Castle acts as Sir Francis Drake's headquarters.

1615 – Town wall completed.

1642 – General Robert Monroe seizes castle for the Scots.

1649 – Royalist garrison surrenders to Cromwell after lengthy siege.

1689 – Frederick, Duke of Schomberg, captures castle for William III.

1690 – William III lands near castle en route to the Battle of the Boyne.

1760 – French troops ransack castle.

1778 – John Paul Jones commands American ship against Britain's HMS *Drake* in naval battle near castle.

1790s – Castle used as a prison.

1928 – Castle passes into State care.

1940s – Castle used as an air-raid shelter.

# Carrickfergus Castle

Overwhelming the basalt dyke below its foundations, Carrickfergus Castle in County Antrim protrudes into Belfast Lough. Almost entirely surrounded by water, this rocky spur provided an ideal platform for a castle. Appreciating its defensive advantages, the Normans swiftly put the site to good use, erecting what is believed to be their earliest stone castle in Ireland to guard the approach to the lough. While its Gaelic name, Carrig Fhearghasa (the Rock of Fergus), remembers the 6th-century drowning of Fergus, the son of Eric of Armoy, the well-preserved castle also stands as a permanent reminder of the Norman invasion of Ireland and the tumult of ensuing centuries.

### The Normans in Northern Ireland

John de Courcy began building a stone fortress at Carrickfergus shortly after storming Ulster in 1177. Over time, his stronghold developed into an imposing triple-enclosure castle dominated, as it is today, by the intimidating three-storey keep. By 1204, when de Courcy, then Lord

**ABOVE:** *Fitted out in the 1560s and again during the Napoleonic Wars for use as an artillery fort, Carrickfergus Castle defended the north-eastern coast of Ireland for well over 800 years.*

**LEFT:** *Although portions of the original gatehouse were demolished to prepare the structure for artillery, the castle chapel remained untouched. Today, its whitewashed walls and decorative carvings add a sense of grace to the heavily militarized stronghold.*

**PREVIOUS PAGE:** *From modest earth-and-timber fortifications to majestic stone fortresses, Ireland is strewn with castles. Mighty Bunratty Castle overlooks the River Shannon as it makes its way to the Atlantic Ocean. Today, the castle welcomes guests to share its medieval atmosphere.*

of Ulster, was forcibly removed from Carrickfergus by Hugh de Lacy, the inner bailey had been enclosed with a polygonal wall. Inside, a great hall occupied the east curtain wall and a 90-foot (27.4-metre) tall rectangular keep commanded the northern corner.

Split into two sections by a cross-wall, the keep's barrel-vaulted basement functioned as a storage area and contained the wellhead. Cross-walls also bisected the upper storeys, which held the public rooms and private accommodation with fireplaces and the lord's latrine. Spiral staircases provided access between the levels.

From 1216 to 1223, when the Crown controlled the castle, workers heightened the keep and moved the great hall from the bailey into the keep. During these years, a series of royal custodians were in charge of the castle, including a man named de Serlane, who was awarded £100 to upgrade the site. De Serlane ordered the construction of another curtain wall, which enclosed a narrow strip of land on the northern and eastern sides of the castle to form the middle bailey.

## Carrickfergus Expands

In 1227 Hugh de Lacy, Earl of Ulster, took possession of Carrickfergus Castle, and doubled its size by enclosing the remainder of the rocky peninsula. Commanded by the powerful twin-towered gatehouse and two lengths of sturdy walling, de Lacy's outer bailey defended the northern approach to the castle. A drawbridge, portcullis and murder holes effectively barred unwanted visitors. Originally, the cylindrical gate-towers stood twice their present height, but during the 16th-century upgrade, labourers demolished the upper levels to accommodate artillery.

Even though the military used Carrickfergus Castle well into the 20th century, the medieval fabric of Ireland's oldest Norman stronghold remained sound. For over eight centuries, the castle suffered siege after siege, but, like the people of Carrickfergus itself, the castle bravely endures the passage of time. Today, the Environment and Heritage Service has responsibility for the castle and opens it to the public throughout the year for a fee.

**BELOW:** *John de Courcy's great keep dominates Carrickfergus Castle completely. Performing dual domestic and military roles, the rectangular structure commanded activity both inside and around the fortress.*

## HISTORY

1269 – Robert de Ufford, justiciar of Ireland, begins castle at Roscommon.

1270s – Hugh O'Connor (O'Conchobair), King of Connaught, destroys castle.

1280s – Rebuilding programme, gatehouse added.

1308 – Donogh O'Kelly gains possession of castle and slays many inhabitants.

1341 – O'Connors re-take castle.

1499 – Garret Mor Fitzgerald, 8th Earl of Kildare, seizes castle.

1569 – Sir Henry Sidney, Elizabeth I's Lord Deputy of Ireland, takes possession.

1578 – Control passes to Sir Nicholas Malby, who remodels castle.

1646 – Surrendered to Irish Confederate forces led by Lieutenant-General Preston.

1652 – Slighted by parliamentarians.

1691 – Destroyed after Battle of Aughrim.

1980s – Roscommon Trust undertakes topographical survey and historical research.

# Roscommon Castle

Roscommon Castle stands in abject ruin, a crumbling shell displaying its original finery, but devastated by warfare and the nuances of time. Nevertheless, this inviting castle possesses a charisma that is created by its piercing mullioned windows and massive round towers. Defended by Ireland's largest twin-towered gatehouse and four powerful corner towers, Roscommon exemplifies the quadrangular castle.

### Low-lying Fortress

One of a spate of quadrangular castles that were erected in Ireland during the late 13th century, Roscommon features elements of Edward I's mighty Welsh fortress at Harlech (see pages 119–21), yet predates it by several years. Unlike Harlech, however, the Irish castle dominates a low-lying marshy site, which made it difficult to replenish, but provided enough water to fill an enclosing moat. A rectangular postern tower projects outward along the western side of the curtain wall. Fitted with a drawbridge and portcullis, the unusual watergate served as a secondary gateway.

As at Harlech, the great twin-towered

gatehouse at Roscommon played a dual role. Much like a keep, it thwarted invasion and also provided accommodation; but its primary function was as the castle's main entrance. Containing an array of defensive mechanisms, the two enormous flanking towers stalwartly guarded the 10-foot (3-metre) wide gate passage. Both gatetowers rose three storeys, their straight-sided back ends protruding well into the inner bailey, which measured 162 by 130 feet (49.4 by 39.6 metres). The gatehouse also housed the castle's largest and most spacious chamber.

Situated at right angles to each corner of the quadrangular wall, the three-storey D-shaped towers provided inhabitants with additional protection as well as living space. Straight staircases rose between each level, which held latrines and fireplaces. The battlemented parapet has long since fallen.

## A Softer Side

In keeping with trends in the late 16th century, Sir Nicholas Malby, Governor of Connaught (Connacht), softened Roscommon Castle's stern military veneer with the addition of mullioned windows and a range of interior domestic buildings. Yet, although the windows allowed light to flood the interiors and created a lace-like façade, the weakened walls became more vulnerable to assault. By the end of the 17th century, the castle had met its match. Cromwell's forces began to dismantle the site in the 1650s, and William III's troops completed the process in 1691. By then, possession of the castle had passed to the earldom of Essex, which continues to own the attractive site to this day.

The Roscommon Millennium Trust presently safeguards the site in association with Dúchas — The Heritage Service. Roscommon Castle is accessible to visitors at any reasonable time.

ABOVE: *The many mullioned windows that were cut into the gatehouse at Roscommon weakened the walls and destabilized the stronghold in the late 16th century.*
OPPOSITE ABOVE: *Added by Sir Nicholas Malby in the late 16th century, this well-preserved mullioned window overlooks the narrow arched passageway through the main gatehouse.*
OPPOSITE: *Protruding outward between two enormous rounded towers cornering the western curtain wall, the unusual rectangular postern tower offered access to and from Roscommon Castle when the main gatehouse was otherwise barricaded.*

## HISTORY

1172 – Hugh de Lacy, 1st Lord of Meath, begins ringwork.

1173 – Rory O'Connor, King of Connaught, burns castle.

1210 – After king's visit, castle known as King John's Castle.

1224 – Masonry castle withstands seven-week siege.

1250s – Geoffrey de Geneville acquires castle upon marrying Maud de Lacy.

1301 – Roger Mortimer, 1st Earl of March, gains castle by right of marriage to Joan, the de Geneville heiress.

1399 – Prince Hal, the future Henry V, and his brother, Humphrey, stay at castle.

1460 – Royal mint established.

15th & 16th centuries – Construction of mantlet, well, corner tower, wash-house with drain and cobbled floors; forebuilding extended.

1534 – Thomas Fitzgerald ('Silken Thomas'), 10th Earl of Kildare, besieges castle.

17th century – Addition of gun emplacements, lead-smelting hearths and blacksmith's forge.

1647 – Catholic Confederate forces storm castle.

1650 – Parliamentarians seize castle.

1970s and 1990s – Archaeological excavations identify ringwork.

# Trim Castle

Situated on the southern bank of the River Boyne, Trim Castle in County Meath casts a medieval shadow over its urban surroundings. Encompassing 3 acres (1.2 hectares) of land, Ireland's largest Norman fortress attests to the strength of the invaders' grip on the kingdom of Meath. Aptly described as Ireland's 'king of castles', King John's Castle symbolizes the dramatic changes imposed by the Normans as they expanded their kingdom across the Irish Sea.

### A Formidable Bastion

It was England's King Henry II who encouraged Hugh de Lacy, his first Lord Lieutenant in Ireland, to construct castles. Henry perceived Richard de Clare, also known as 'Strongbow' (c. 1130–76), who led the Norman invasion of Ireland, as a threat to the throne, and wanted to keep his rival in check. Trim Castle became de Lacy's base. From here, he could guard movement along the River Boyne, receive supplies directly into the castle from the port of Drogheda and control the region as far west as Athlone, which overlooked the River Shannon.

After withstanding an assault on the castle by Connaught's High King, Rory O'Connor, in 1173, de Lacy recognized the weaknesses in the ringwork's timber defences. He swiftly embarked on a building programme that ultimately converted the simple stronghold into a formidable enclosure castle. In its final form, Trim Castle consisted of a triangular curtain wall, its southern side fitted at intervals with D-shaped towers. The blocky Dublin gateway and barbican also faced southwards, towards Ireland's capital city. The main gatehouse bisected the western curtain wall, and the now ruined eastern side, which commanded the river, supported the royal mint, three square towers, an impressive great hall and storage facilities. Two watergates opened to slipways and allowed access to the river below.

### Cruciform Keep

Planted inside the ringwork castle's earthen embankments, Trim's imposing Norman keep exacts attention. A variant of the classic rectangular keep, this massive cruciform building is the only one of its kind in Ireland. Centred by a 76-foot (23-metre) high square core that stretches 65 feet (19.8 metres) across, the remarkable structure featured four square towers, each of which projected outwards mid-way along each side. When completed, the great keep was three storeys high, contained living quarters with fireplaces, a chapel and a hall on the third floor which was accessed by a wooden stairway.

A deep ditch carved from the underlying bedrock provided a substantial obstacle to any enemy attempt to undermine the keep. Direct assault was possible only if attackers managed to breach the heavily defended main gateway, cross the drawbridge that spanned the ditch and then storm the forebuilding, which opened into the first storey of the keep.

ABOVE: *Trim's complex keep features a variety of structures, including a public hall, the lord's great chambers, a chapel and other accommodation. Staircases within the walls of two turrets eased movement.*

OPPOSITE: *On the River Boyne, Ireland's largest castle at Trim dominates its surroundings completely. Encompassed by the great gatehouse and multi-towered curtain wall, the keep was virtually indestructible.*

## Hidden History

During the 18th and 19th centuries, Trim's powerful castle lost its final battle. Locals pilfered the masonry for building material and probably burned the stone in lime kilns in the inner bailey. Nonetheless, excavations have revealed the hidden history of the great fortress, including physical evidence of a burnt building inside the ringwork. Archaeologists have also unearthed horseshoes, arrowheads, a wine jug and a cache of human burials.

Now managed by Dúchas – The Heritage Service, Trim Castle has undergone extensive conservation. It is open to the public during the summer months for an entrance fee. Despite the presence of modern buildings all too close to its lush green grounds, this historic riverside fortress pays everlasting tribute to Ireland's turbulent past.

LEFT: *One of three main entry points into the castle, Trim Gate looked westwards towards the town.*

BELOW: *Trim's great cruciform keep was probably built in two separate phases, beginning in about 1200. The powerful structure could function as a self-sufficient unit in wartime and as a comfortable home in peacetime.*

# Bunratty Castle

Using historical documents to accurately renovate his castle, Viscount Lord Gort began Bunratty Castle's renaissance in the 1950s. Now restored inside and out, Ireland's largest and grandest tower house vividly introduces visitors to life in the late Middle Ages, when clan fought clan and also struggled for freedom against an increasingly pervasive English monarchy. Both physically and historically, the monumental tower house in County Clare reflects Ireland's history of revolt against occupation. The castle's story began with the Normans, who erected a motte castle at the site in the 13th century, and continued through to the 19th century, when the last Plantation family (the English and Scottish settlers who had been imposed on Irish land seized by the English monarchy) finally moved out. Fortunately, Lord Gort had the foresight to rescue the impressive site.

**BELOW:** *Bunratty Castle is one of Ireland's grandest tower houses. The battlemented structure rises five storeys and displays matching twin-towered façades meant to confuse attackers.*

**ABOVE:** *The ornate great hall features exquisite tapestries and paintings, fine furniture, such as the Chair of Estate, and lovely stained-glass panels.*

## HISTORY

AD 970 – Vikings occupy site.

1250 – Robert de Muscegros constructs earth-and-timber fortress.

1270s – Thomas de Clare builds masonry castle.

1318 – Irish of Thomond destroy castle and town; English rebuild.

1332 – Irish, led by O'Briens and MacNamaras, destroy Bunratty Castle.

1353 – Sir Thomas Rokeby, Justiciar of Ireland, rebuilds; Irish seize castle.

1425 – MacNamaras begin tower house.

1475 – O'Briens, Kings of Thomond, take over castle.

1543 – Henry VIII creates O'Briens as Earls of Thomond.

1646 – Papal nuncio, Archbishop Rinuccini, visits 6th Earl of Thomond; 6th Earl surrenders to Admiral Penn, Commonwealth commander.

1804 – The Studdarts, a Plantation family, abandon castle in favour of Bunratty House.

1954 – 7th Viscount Lord Gort purchases castle; begins restoration programme.

1976 – Upon Lord Gort's death, castle passes into State care.

rises for four storeys. Each level contains a single large chamber. The first-floor entrance leads directly into a vaulted hall, known as the main guard, which displays an enchanting minstrels' gallery. The hall once serviced the garrison and provided added protection for the resident lord. On the storey above, the Earls of Thomond held court and entertained guests in their splendid great hall, where fine tapestries and paintings adorned the walls. A brazier heated the entire chamber, and louvres in the ceiling allowed smoke to escape overhead.

Each corner tower measures over 23 square feet (2.1 square metres) and features narrow windows, a staircase and a battlemented roof line. Inside, the five-storey towers held the castle's main accommodation. Besides private apartments, the towers contained chambers for the captain of the guard, the kitchen, special rooms for the castle priest, a private chapel and a public chapel; the latter is particularly noteworthy for its lovely stucco ceiling. A discreetly located window in the north solar allowed the earl and his family to observe the action in the great hall.

Bunratty's impressive tower house, lush gardens and adjoining park, which once sustained

ABOVE: *Situated immediately below the priest's room, the authentically furnished public, or lower, chapel harkens to its medieval origins. Of particular note are the 15th-century altarpiece and the ornate plasterwork ceiling, which dates to the 16th century.*

## High Tower House

Bunratty Castle consists of a rectangular core fronted north and south with bulky façades, each of which is flanked by two enormous corner towers. High arches span the void between the towers, linking them together. The effect is remarkably similar to Hermitage Castle (see pages 74–6), the great Scottish tower house erected in the 14th century, but Bunratty stands much taller. Measuring 62 by 41 feet (19 by 12.5 metres), Bunratty's central tower

over 3,000 deer, undoubtedly brought great pleasure to the MacNamaras, who built the castle, and to the O'Briens, Earls of Thomond, who lived there in splendour for almost 200 years. Now largely refurbished, Bunratty Castle continues to charm modern visitors.

Shannon Development now manages Bunratty Castle as part of the Bunratty Folk Park. It is open to the public throughout the year for a fee, and visitors can also take part in medieval banquets.

# Limerick Castle

As early as 1175, the Normans established a base at Limerick, which had previously been a possession of the O'Briens, Kings of Thomond. From their earth-and-timber fortification, the outsiders capably commanded their environs. Within 40 years, their ringwork castle developed into one of Ireland's most substantial stone-enclosure castles. Today, Limerick Castle's massive round towers emerge from the waters of the River Shannon, as it sweeps past King's Island, from where it once commanded all passage along the river.

## King John's Castle

One of several strongholds to claim the name King John's Castle, Limerick's five-sided, five-towered fortress served as the region's military and administrative centre. From the royal stronghold, the English king intended not only to subdue the Irish, but also to prevent potential rivals, his own Norman overlords, from expanding their holdings. The transformation into stone occurred during John's reign, when the polygonal curtain wall replaced the ringwork's stone-revetted ramparts. At the same time, construction began on medieval walls to defend English Town, which occupied the 200-acre (80-hectare) island and enclosed the castle, and also around Irish Town, which developed on the mainland.

BELOW: *Among its varied roles, Limerick Castle operated a royal mint, where silver coinage was manufactured. Located in the north-western tower, the mint has been restored to its medieval appearance.*

ABOVE: *Fronting the gatehouse, twin stone cylinders guard the main entrance into Limerick Castle. The structure served as the constable's residence.*

## HISTORY

1175 – Ringwork castle erected.

1205 – Masonry construction begins.

13th century – Walls of English Town erected; construction of great hall.

1310 – Walling of Irish Town.

1316 – Edward Bruce captures castle.

1332 – O'Briens, Earls of Desmond, seize castle, but local citizenry take over.

1585 – Castle in decay.

1608 – Military engineer Sir Josias Bodley adds south-east bastion to support heavy artillery.

1642 – Irish assault forces garrison to surrender.

1651 – Irish surrender to parliamentarian troops led by General Henry Ireton.

1690 – William III's army besieges castle.

1691 – Patrick Sarsfield, Earl of Lucan, surrenders to William's troops.

1751 – Barracks built.

1760 – Demolition of medieval walls begins.

1842 – Viscount Lord Gort, castle constable, dies.

1922 – British army withdraws.

1935 – Limerick Corporation builds 22 houses on castle grounds.

1989 – Houses demolished; restoration process begins.

1990s – Archaeological excavations reveal remains of ringwork castle and great hall.

RIGHT: *When viewed from the inner bailey, the flat-backed twin gatehouse towers lose their menacing character. Yet, along with the drawbridge and a sturdy portcullis, the main gate fulfilled its defensive role capably.*

BELOW: *Poised to overlook the southern banks of the River Shannon immediately alongside the Thomond Bridge, King John's powerful castle functioned as an administrative and military centre for English forces in Ireland.*

Adjacent to the castle, the Thomond Bridge facilitated movement between the two towns, as it does today.

### Before Its Time

Everything about Limerick Castle radiates domination and power. The strategic use of round towers at the corners and on either side of the main entrance demonstrates a technological sophistication normally associated with Edward I's castle-building efforts in the late 13th century, but Limerick Castle had already achieved its final shape by the end of the 12th century.

For four centuries, Limerick Castle stood virtually unaltered. Then, in the 17th century, Sir George Carew, Lord President of Munster (1555–1629), ordered defensive improvements to accommodate artillery. His most significant contribution, a large bastion supporting cannons at the south-eastern corner, no longer stands. The modern visitor centre, which showcases recent archaeological discoveries, now occupies the spot.

Today, Shannon Development manages Limerick Castle. Unsightly houses built in the inner bailey earlier in the 20th century have been demolished, and the castle has recaptured its medieval character through an extensive consolidation programme. Restoration work on the town walls has also been ongoing. Limerick's castle and medieval walls remain tangible symbols of the divisiveness and perseverance that have shaped the course of Ireland's history. The castle is open throughout the year for an entrance fee.

# Rock of Cashel

The unsuspecting traveller may be forgiven for gasping at the mass of brown masonry that surges abruptly into view, protruding from an otherwise flat plain that is appropriately named the Golden Vein. Legend has it that, startled by the sight of St Patrick converting sinners on the ground below, the devil, who happened to be overhead at the time, dropped an enormous limestone rock onto the spot. Even today, the vision of the jumbled ruins silhouetted against the bright Irish sun has the unnerving ability to startle passers-by. Fortified by the kings of Munster, Tipperary's Rock of Cashel developed from a primitive stone fortress into one of Ireland's most important ecclesiastical centres. A stronghold of kings and bishops and a scene of battle and rebirth, this cluster of ancient structures merges the past with the present and reflects the best of Irish history.

**BELOW:** *The Rock of Cashel radiates mystery and majesty as if it has merged with the craggy ridge underneath its foundations. This site is one of Ireland's most historic and beautiful treasures.*

**ABOVE:** *Grave slabs scatter the floor inside the nave of the ruined 13th-century cathedral, which replaced the earlier church erected by Donal Mor O'Brien.*

## HISTORY

4th century AD – Eoghanachta clan from Wales (Kings of Munster, later the McCarthys) fortify site.

5th century – St Patrick visits Cashel, converts King Aenghus to Christianity.

970s – O'Briens, led by Brian Boru, High King of Ireland, acquire site.

1101 – King Muircheartach O'Brien grants site to Church.

1127 – Cormac McCarthy erects chapel.

1169 – Donal Mor O'Brien, King of Limerick, begins cathedral.

1172 – Irish clergy pay homage to Henry II.

1260s – New cathedral begun.

15th century – Tower house and Hall of Vicars Choral added.

1647 – Parliamentarian troops led by Lord Inchiquin seize site.

1975 – Restoration begins on Hall of the Vicars Choral.

**LEFT:** *Pointing to the heavens, Cashel's marvellous round tower provided defensive support for the normally peaceful inhabitants of the Rock. Scattered throughout the Irish countryside, such striking towers are among medieval Ireland's most characteristic architectural forms.*

**BELOW LEFT:** *Fragments of an ornate stone sarcophagus found in Cormac's Chapel contain classical examples of early medieval scrollwork and stylized designs, for which Ireland is famous.*

**OPPOSITE:** *Entirely occupying the jagged limestone crag upon which it was built, the mass of buildings that together comprise the complex known as the Rock of Cashel includes both religious and secular structures.*

## Muddled Monument

Rising 100 feet (30 metres) above the countryside, the Rock of Cashel dominates it surroundings completely. Used continuously from the 4th century, the site takes its name from the Gaelic *Caiseal Mumhan*, which means 'the stone fort of Munster'. Structures from virtually every major building phase in Ireland's history form what seems to be more a maze of masonry than an organized complex of buildings. Not surprisingly, visitors may find the monument confusing to negotiate.

Ringed by a powerful stone wall, the Rock of Cashel consists of five main buildings, haunting Celtic crosses in the adjoining graveyard and a museum displaying fragile artefacts.

A classic example of its kind, the well-preserved cylindrical round tower dates to the early 12th century, making it the rock's oldest surviving structure. Built to protect the clerics who lived there from sudden attack, the tower stands 92 feet (28 metres) tall. A fine Norman doorway offered access to the tower about 10 feet (3 metres) above ground. Remains of the extensively ruined 13th-century cathedral can be identified close to the round tower. Cruciform in plan, the cathedral once featured a long choir, a central tower, a short nave and chapels in each transept; it still houses several interesting tombs.

## Cormac's Chapel

Consecrated in 1134, Cormac's Chapel has achieved widespread renown for its intricate ornamentation and quality architecture. Begun by Cormac McCarthy (MacCarthaigh) in

1127, the small chapel features a barrel-vaulted roof, twin towers, medieval paintings and an eye-catching tympanum that displays skilfully carved creatures and human heads. A well-preserved stone sarcophagus, which is said to be the tomb of King Cormac himself, dominates the interior of the chapel.

In the 15th century, the Rock of Cashel acquired its final form when builders added the Hall of the Vicars Choral, which was constructed for a group of eight laymen or minor canons whose primary role was to chant during services, and a tower house. Today, the Hall of the Vicars Choral houses a museum. The tower house, on the other hand, has decayed greatly over the centuries, and is barely distinguishable among the ruins. Constructed at the end of the cathedral nave, possibly to replace the cramped round tower, the thick-walled rectangular tower house stood 73 feet tall (22.2 metres), measured 41 by 28½ feet (12.5 by 8.7 metres), and was riddled with passages. Whether or not the clerics ever put the arrow slits to good use remains a mystery.

### Pilgrimage Site

Now managed by Dúchas – The Heritage Service, the Rock of Cashel draws pilgrims to the site throughout the year. Whether visitors seek spiritual solace or a connection with the past, the conglomeration of religious and secular buildings inevitably sparks their curiosity and admiration. It is open throughout the year for an entrance fee.

# Kilkenny Castle

## HISTORY

1172 – Richard de Clare, Earl of Pembroke, erects earth-and-timber castle.

1174 – Donald (Domhnall) O'Brien, King of Thomond, destroys castle.

1207 – William Marshal begins masonry castle.

1366 – Statutes of Kilkenny attempt to segregate the native Irish and English inhabitants of Ireland.

1391 – James Butler, 3rd Earl of Ormonde, purchases castle.

1642–48 – Confederation of Kilkenny meets at castle.

1650 – Parliamentarians besiege castle; James Butler, 12th Earl, flees into exile with Prince Charles, son of the recently executed king; garrison surrenders after five days.

1659 – Fourth drum tower destroyed during remodelling.

1660s and 1670s – Major restoration programme.

1690 – James Butler, 2nd Duke of Ormonde, entertains William III at castle.

1716 – 2nd Duke flees to France and is convicted of treason in absentia for supporting the Jacobites and forced to give up the castle.

1758 – After death of last male heir, castle begins to decay.

1766 – Walter Butler of Garryricken inherits title and moves into castle; adds stables, Butler House, landscaping.

1820s – James Butler, 19th Earl and 1st Marquess of Ormonde, hires William Robertson to 're-medievalize' castle.

1850s – James Butler, 3rd Marquess, adds Moorish staircase, sham battlements, castellated towers.

1922 – Anti-Treatyites seize castle, but surrender after two days.

1935 – Ormondes auction furnishings and move away from castle, which decays.

1967 – Arthur Butler, 6th Marquess and 23rd Earl of Ormonde, sells castle to city, which places it into State care.

Second in importance only to medieval Dublin Castle, Kilkenny Castle and its owners played a key role in shaping Ireland's history. Situated immediately above the banks of the River Nore, the unusual trapezoid-shaped enclosure castle reflects changing attitudes, circumstances and owners.

### The Butlers' Castle

Replacing a Celtic settlement that had been established by St Canice (Cainaeach) in the 6th century AD, Richard de Clare 'Strongbow' built an earth-and-timber castle at the site shortly after his initial foray into Ireland. Accompanying Strongbow on the invasion were the FitzWalters, who changed their surname to Butler (le Botiller) in 1185, when Henry II, the English king, appointed Theobald FitzWalter as Chief Butler of Ireland. FitzWalter had the honour of presenting the new king with his first cup of wine and had the responsibility

of levying taxes ('butlerage') on all imported wines. The Butlers made Kilkenny Castle their permanent home in 1391.

In 1207, Strongbow's son-in-law, William Marshal, Earl of Pembroke, began the timber castle's transformation into a substantial masonry fortress defended by four powerful round towers, which were the Marshal trademark design and which were also found at the Welsh castles of Pembroke (see pages 116–18) and Chepstow (see pages 106–109). When completed, the great stone trapezoid would have entirely enclosed the inner bailey, but now only three sides of the original quadrangle and three of the corner towers still stand. The strange layout forms a modified C-plan and gives Kilkenny the appearance of a work in progress. Yet, records from 1307 document that the castle had a hall, four towers, a chapel, a moat and other buildings, which indicates that the present structure resembles, at least in plan, its medieval predecessor.

## Welcoming Monarchs

Over the course of its history, Kilkenny developed from an inhospitable fortress into an impressive castellated residence that welcomed several royal guests, including Anne Boleyn and kings Charles I, William III, Edward VII, George V and their queens. The Butlers' collection of fine tapestries and paintings hangs on the walls of the long gallery. Nearby, an ornate chimney piece displays their heraldic emblems. Other notable features include a lavish staircase, library, drawing room and bedrooms that are decorated as they may have been during the 1830s. The lovely interiors remember a grander age, when the castle served as the seat of the Earls of Ormonde and also as the seat of the Irish government during times of crisis.

Now managed by Dúchas – The Heritage Service, Kilkenny Castle is open to the public throughout the year for an entrance fee.

OPPOSITE ABOVE: *No longer needing a human garrison, the walled courtyard enclosing Kilkenny Castle now features stoic stone warriors as its army.*

OPPOSITE BELOW: *Restored to reflect the grandeur of the Marshal Earls of Pembroke and the Butler Earls of Ormonde, the beauty of the Long Gallery is incomparable.*

BELOW: *Despite experiencing several rebuilding programmes over the centuries, trapezoidal Kilkenny Castle retains much of William Marshal's 13th-century design.*

# Cahir Castle

## HISTORY

**3rd century AD** – The earthen Dun Iascaigh ('town of the fish fort') occupies site.

**12th century** – Conor Na Cathrach O'Brien, King of Thomond, fortifies site.

**1192** – Philip of Worcester acquires barony of Cahir.

**13th century** – Construction begins.

**1375** – Castle becomes seat of James Butler, 3rd Earl of Ormonde.

**1405** – James Butler, the 3rd Earl's illegitimate son, also known as James 'the Foreigner' (Seamus Gallda), begins major building programme.

**1543** – Thomas Butler becomes Lord Baron of Cahir.

**1647** – George Mathews, Lord Cahir's guardian, surrenders castle to parliamentarian leader, Murrogh O'Brien, Lord Inchiquin.

**1650** – Oliver Cromwell takes castle.

**1652** – Butlers resume possession of castle.

**1662** – Butlers move to Rehill House.

**1770s** – Butlers abandon castle in favour of Cahir House.

**1816** – Richard Butler of Glengall becomes 1st Earl of Glengall.

**1840s** – Richard Butler, 2nd Earl, restores castle.

**1860s** – Construction of Cahir Park.

**1961** – Last heir, Richard Butler Charteris, dies.

**1964** – Castle passes into State care.

Described to Elizabeth I as 'the only famous castle in Ireland which is thought impregnable', the aptly named stronghold at Cahir (*cathair* means 'stone fort') boldly commands its watery surroundings as it would have done during the queen's reign. Erected on a limestone rock washed on all sides by the River Suir, which was navigable to this point, Cahir Castle provided a crucial link between Waterford and Limerick. Within 200 years of its founding, the castle developed from a rudimentary stone fort into one of Ireland's largest and most impressive medieval fortresses.

### Cahir Through the Ages

Cahir Castle is a fascinating site consisting of three main areas, each representing a different phase in its history. Now encompassing the inner bailey, the 13th-century Norman castle occupied the highest point on the limestone island. Always the most complex part of the development, the inner bailey featured strong towers at each corner and an enormous gatehouse that overlooked the southern side of the island, which was not yet fortified.

Commanding the north-western corner of the Norman castle, the three-storey keep acted as the original strongpoint. Fitted with latrines that dumped into the river and private accommodation on the upper levels, the imposing rectangular tower suited the military and domestic needs of the lord. Stairs next to the square north-eastern tower led down into the round well tower, a curious structure that projected outwards from the curtain wall to penetrate the waters of the Suir.

In the 15th century, James 'the Foreigner' Butler altered the layout of the fortress and converted the rectangular gatehouse into a primary residence, akin to a keep-gatehouse. Separating the rectangular twin-towers, the central passageway originally allowed access into the inner bailey from the south. When Butler gained possession of Cahir Castle, he blocked the gate passage and moved the main entrance to an arched gap just to the east. At the same time, he also enclosed the remainder of the island, creating a spacious outer bailey with two round towers to watch the southern approach. During the 16th century, the lords of Cahir added a cross-wall to the northern end of the outer bailey. The newly enclosed open area became known as the middle bailey.

## Damage, Disrepair and Debt

Despite contemporary boasts of impregnability, Robert Devereux, Earl of Essex (1566–1601), who was one of Queen Elizabeth's favourite courtiers, damaged the formidable castle extensively during a 10-day siege in 1599. Fortunately, the tattered stronghold experienced a renaissance in the 1840s, when Richard Butler, 1st Earl of Glengall, began to restore his ancestral home. However, the Butlers found themselves in serious financial straits by the end of the decade, and were forced to declare bankruptcy and sell off much of their property to cover the debts.

In the late 1870s, Lady Margaret Butler Charteris re-acquired the Cahir estates, and the empty castle remained with the family until 1961. While modern development has consumed much of the town, the fully consolidated castle at Cahir remains the Butlers' lasting and grandest legacy. Its militarized façade contrasts with the softer, more regal appearance presented by the Butlers' castle at Kilkenny (see pages 152–3). Today, Cahir Castle is managed by Dúchas – The Heritage Service, and is open throughout the year for an entrance fee.

ABOVE: *Cahir Castle's original keep stands at the north-western corner of inner bailey, poised to watch over the activity on the River Suir. To the east, the squat well tower plunges to the river, which served as the castle's water supply.*

OPPOSITE ABOVE: *Added in the 15th century during the conversion of the main gatehouse into the great keep, the smaller inner gateway was defended with a portcullis and machicolations, which projected outwards so that guards could drop missiles on unsuspecting attackers.*

OPPOSITE BELOW: *Hubbing the stone-enclosure castle, the great tower dominates the centre of the site. It functioned as the main gate into the inner bailey until the addition of the outer bailey in the 15th century.*

# CONTACT DETAILS

## THE GREAT CASTLES OF ENGLAND

**Carlisle Castle**
Carlisle, Cumbria
CA3 8UR
Tel: 01228 591922
www.english-heritage.org.uk

**Bamburgh Castle**
Bamburgh, Northumberland
NE69 7DF
Tel: 01668 214515
www.bamburghcastle.com

**Alnwick Castle**
Alnwick, Northumberland
NE66 1NQ
Tel: 01665 511100
www.alnwickcastle.com

**Warkworth Castle**
Morpeth, Northumberland
NE65 0UJ
Tel: 01665 711423

**Kenilworth Castle**
Kenilworth, Warwickshire
CV8 1NE
Tel: 01926 852078
www.english-heritage.org.uk

**Warwick Castle**
Warwick, Warwickshire
CV34 4QU
Tel: 0870 4422000
www.warwick-castle.co.uk

**Conisbrough Castle**
Castle Hill, Conisbrough,
Doncaster DN12 3BU
Tel: 01709 863329
www.english-heritage.org.uk

**Goodrich Castle**
Goodrich, Ross-on-Wye,
Herefordshire HR9 6HY
Tel: 01600 890538
www.english-heritage.org.uk

**Berkeley Castle**
Berkeley, Gloucestershire
GL13 9BQ
Tel: 01453 810332
www.berkeley-castle.com

**Corfe Castle**
Wareham, Dorset
BH20 5EZ
Tel: 01929 481294
www.nationaltrust.org.uk

**Castle Rising Castle**
Castle Rising,
King's Lynn, Norfolk
PE31 6AH
Tel: 01553 631330

**Windsor Castle**
Windsor, Berkshire
SL4 1NJ
Tel: 01753 868286
www.royal.gov.uk

**Tower of London**
Tower Hill, London
EC3N 4AB
Tel: 020 7709 0765
www.hrp.org.uk

**Rochester Castle**
Rochester, Kent ME1 1SW
Tel: 01634 402276
www.english-heritage.org.uk

**Dover Castle**
Dover, Kent CT16 1HU
Tel: 01304 211067
www.english-heritage.org.uk

**Bodiam Castle**
Bodiam, Robertsbridge, East
Sussex TN32 5UA
Tel: 01580 830436
www.nationaltrust.org.uk

**Arundel Castle**
Arundel, West Sussex
BN18 9AB
Tel: 01903 882173
www.arundelcastle.org

**Restormel Castle**
Lostwithiel, Cornwall
PL22 0DB
Tel: 01208 872687
www.english-heritage.org.uk

## THE GREAT CASTLES OF SCOTLAND

**Caerlaverock Castle**
Glencaple, Dumfries,
Dumfries & Galloway
DG1 4RU
Tel: 01387 770244
www.historic-scotland.gov.uk

**Threave Castle**
Castle Douglas, Dumfries &
Galloway DG7 1RX
Tel: 07711 223101
www.historic-scotland.gov.uk

**Edinburgh Castle**
Castlehill, Edinburgh
EH1 2NG
Tel: 0131 2259846
www.historic-scotland.gov.uk

**Stirling Castle**
Stirling, Stirlingshire
FK8 1EJ
Tel: 01786 450000
www.historic-scotland.gov.uk

**Bothwell Castle**
Castle Avenue, Bothwell,
Uddingston, Glasgow
G71 8BL
Tel: 01698 816894
www.historic-scotland.gov.uk

**Rothesay Castle**
Castlehill Street, Rothesay,
Isle of Bute PA20 0DA
Tel: 01700 502691
www.historic-scotland.gov.uk

**Claypotts Castle**
Broughty Ferry, Dundee
DD5 3JY
Tel: 01786 450000
www.historic-scotland.gov.uk

**Hermitage Castle**
Liddlesdale, Newcastleton,
Borders TD9 0LU
Tel: 01387 376222

**Dunnottar Castle**
The Dunnottar Trust
Estates Office, Dunecht,
Westhill, Aberdeenshire
AB32 7AW
Tel: 01569 762173
www.dunechtestates.co.uk

**Glamis Castle**
Glamis, Forfar, Angus
DD8 1RJ
Tel: 01307 840393
www.glamis-castle.co.uk

**Urquhart Castle**
Drumnadrochit,
Invernessshire IV63 6SJ
Tel: 01456 450551
www.historic-scotland.gov.uk

**Eilean Donan Castle**
Dornie, near Kyle of
Lochalsh, Ross-shire
IV40 8DX
Tel: 01599 555202
www.eileandonancastle.com

**Dunvegan Castle**
Isle of Skye IV55 8WF
Tel: 01470 521206
www.dunvegancastle.com

## THE GREAT CASTLES OF WALES

**Chepstow Castle**
Bridge Street, Chepstow,
Monmouthshire
NP6 5EZ
Tel: 01291 624065
www.cadw.wales.gov.uk

**White Castle**
Llantilio Crossenny,
Abergavenny,
Monmouthshire
NP7 8UD
Tel: 01600 780380
www.cadw.wales.gov.uk

**Raglan Castle**
Raglan, Gwent NP5 2BT
Tel: 01291 690228
www.cadw.wales.gov.uk

**Caerphilly Castle**
Caerphilly CF83 1JD
Tel: 02920 883143
www.cadw.wales.gov.uk

**Pembroke Castle**
Pembroke, Pembrokeshire
SA71 4LA
Tel: 01646 681510
www.pembrokecastle.co.uk

**Kidwelly Castle**
Kidwelly, Carmarthenshire
SA17 5BG
Tel: 01554 890104
www.cadw.wales.gov.uk

**Dolwyddelan Castle**
Dolwyddelan, Conwy
Tel: 01690 750366
www.cadw.wales.gov.uk

**Caernarfon Castle**
Caernarfon, Gwynedd
LL55 2AY
Tel: 01286 677617
www.cadw.wales.gov.uk

**Beaumaris Castle**
Beaumaris, Anglesey
LL58 8AP
Tel: 01248 810361
www.cadw.wales.gov.uk

**Harlech Castle**
Castle Square, Harlech,
Gwynedd LL46 2YH
Tel: 01766 780552
www.cadw.wales.gov.uk

**Conwy Castle**
Rose Hill Street, Conwy
LL32 8LD
Tel: 01492 592358
www.cadw.wales.gov.uk

**Rhuddlan Castle**
Castle Street, Rhuddlan,
Rhyl, Denbighshire
LL18 5AD
Tel: 01745 590777
www.cadw.wales.gov.uk

## THE GREAT CASTLES OF IRELAND

**Carrickfergus Castle**
Marine Highway,
Carrickfergus, Co. Antrim
BT38 7BG
Tel: 028 9335 1273
www.ehsni.gov.uk

**Roscommon Castle**
Castle Street, Roscommon,
Co. Roscommon
Tel:+353 90 6626342
(tourist office)

**Trim Castle**
Trim, Co. Meath
Tel: + 353 46 9438619
www.heritageireland.ie

**Bunratty Castle**
Bunratty, Co. Clare
Tel: +353 61 360788
www.shannonheritage.com

**Limerick Castle**
King John's Island,
Nicholas Street, Limerick,
Co. Limerick
Tel: +353 61 411201

**Rock of Cashel**
Cashel, Co. Tipperary
Tel: +353 62 61437
www.heritageireland.ie

**Kilkenny Castle**
Kilkenny, Co. Kilkenny
Tel: +353 56 7721450
www.heritageireland.ie

**Cahir Castle**
Castle Street, Cahir, Co.
Tipperary
Tel: +353 52 41011
www.heritageireland.ie

# GLOSSARY

**Arrow slit:** vertical slot in a wall for firing arrows from inside castle; also known as arrow loop.

**Aumbry:** cupboard for storing valuables.

**Bailey:** defended courtyard or ward.

**Barbican:** fortified outwork defending the gate of a castle or town.

**Bartizan:** overhanging corner turret.

**Battery:** gun emplacement.

**Battlement:** jagged stonework protecting the wall-walk; also known as crenellation.

**Belfry:** wooden siege tower mounted on wheels or rollers.

**Burh:** Anglo-Saxon defended settlement.

**Caponier:** covered connecting passageway.

**Casemate:** vaulted chamber embedded in ramparts or walls and equipped with a gun emplacement; passageway within thickness of a curtain wall that leads to gun and musket ports.

**Cat:** hide-covered framework that protected miners during a siege.

**Constable:** castle governor.

**Corbel:** projecting feature used to support an overhanging parapet, platform, turret or timber beams.

**Crenellation:** see battery.

**Curtain:** defensive wall enclosing a bailey, generally constructed in stone.

**Dais:** a raised platform at the end of the great hall for the lord's table.

**Ditch:** dry moat encircling castle.

**Donjon:** keep or great tower.

**Drawbridge:** bridge or roadway across a moat or ditch that lifted or pivoted to prevent unwanted access.

**Enceinte:** enclosure or courtyard wall.

**Flying arch:** a stone archway spanning a gap between two walls or towers.

**Flying buttress:** a free-standing buttress or stone support, attached to the main structure by an arch or a half-arch and often elaborately carved; typically associated with Gothic architecture.

**Forework:** a masonry or earthen structure erected outside the main gateway to bolster the castle's defences; see barbican, revetment

**Garderobe:** latrine chute, privy or castle toilet.

**Garret:** top floor or attic room.

**Gatehouse:** strong multi-storey structure containing a fortified gate, portcullis chamber and accommodation for the constable.

**Great hall:** entertainment centre of the castle where guests were feasted; also used as the administrative chamber.

**Gun emplacement:** platform or defended position providing a place to secure cannons or other guns for firing.

**Hornwork:** outer earthwork barrier usually set before an entrance to impede attackers.

**Keep:** a self-sufficient, fortified tower containing living quarters and used as the last line of refuge in a siege. Also explain shell keep.

**Machicolations:** openings in the floor of a projecting parapet or platform, located along a wall or above an archway, through which defenders could drop or shoot missiles vertically onto attackers below; functioned similar to murder holes.

**Magazine:** chamber for storing ammunition, arms and provisions.

**Moat:** water-filled ditch encircling the castle.

**Murder holes:** openings in the ceiling of a gate passage through which missiles and liquids could be hurled onto attackers or fires.

**Palisade:** timber fencing, normally placed on top of earthen ramparts or motte.

**Parapet:** a protective, battlemented wall facing the outer side of the wall-walk

**Portcullis:** heavy wooden, iron or combination grille protecting an entrance.

**Putlog holes:** holes left by the withdrawal of scaffolding.

**Rampart:** battlement or protected fighting platform; a defensive bank of earth or rubble, topped with timber fence.

**Range:** a group of associated buildings.

**Redoubt:** square or polygonal earthwork used to temporarily fortify a spot.

**Revetment:** an outwork or embankment faced with a layer of timber or masonry.

**Sapper:** a skilled labourer who excavates an underground tunnel, propping up walls and ceilings along the way with timber to prevent premature collapse.

**Siege engine:** timber machine for firing missiles at castle or for scaling walls.

**Slighting:** the process of rendering a castle useless to prevent its future use.

**Solar:** lord's private living quarters, usually adjacent to great hall; a withdrawing chamber.

**Springald:** siege engine resembling a giant crossbow.

**Thanage:** area controlled by a thane; also spelled thaneage.

**Trebuchet:** stone-throwing siege engine worked with counterweights.

**Turret:** a small tower, often an addition to a larger tower.

**Twin-towered:** describing a gatehouse with matching towers that flank each side of the gate passage.

**Undermining:** digging a tunnel at the base of a curtain wall or tower, which is then propped up with timber beams and set alight to bring down the foundations overhead.

**Wall-walk:** interior walkway along a wall top protected by a parapet.

# FURTHER READING

Coventry, Martin (2001). *The Castles of Scotland*. Musselburgh: Goblinshead.
Creighton, Oliver and Robert Higham (2003). *Medieval Castles*. Princes Risborough: Shire Publications Ltd.
Donnelly, Mark P & Daniel Diehl (1998) *Siege: Castles at War*. Dallas: Taylor Publishing Company.
Fry, Plantagenet Somerset (1996). *Castles of Britain and Ireland*. New York & London: Abbeville Press Publishers.
Kenyon, John R (1990). *Medieval Fortifications*. Leicester & London: Leicester University Press.

Kenyon, John R & Kieran O'Conor, eds. (2003). *The Medieval Castle in Ireland and Wales*. Dublin: Four Courts Press Ltd.
Platt, Colin (1996). *The Castle in Medieval England & Wales*. New York: Barnes & Noble.
Sweetman, David (1999). *The Medieval Castles of Ireland*. Woodbridge: Boydell & Brewer Ltd.
Warner, Philip (1993). *The Medieval Castle: Life in a Fortress in Peace and War*. New York: Barnes & Noble.

# INDEX

Page numbers in **bold** refer to main references and illustrations.
Page numbers in *italics* refer to illustrations/captions

Aberystwyth Castle 134
Adam, Robert 22, 24
Adeliza de Louvain 29, 43, 59
Aenghus, King 149
Albany, Murdoch Stewart, 2nd Duke of 71
Albert Edward, Prince of Wales 124
Albert, Prince 43, 45, 49
Albini, William d' (13th century) 51
Albini, William d', Earl of Sussex 29, 59
Alexander II of Scotland 18, 22, 92
Alexander III of Scotland 92
Alnwick Castle 7, **22–4**
Anglo-Saxons 20, 52, 53
Angus, Dame Margaret Maxwell, Countess of 82
Anne of Cleves 50
Argyle, Archibald, 9th Earl of 99
Armstrong family 20
Arundel, Edmund, 2nd Earl of 59
Arundel, Richard Fitzalan, 1st Earl of 59
Arundel Castle 9, 11, 16, *17*, **59–60**
Arundell, Sir Ralph 64
Ashcombe, George Cubitt, Lord 56

baileys 6, 8, 9, 11, 102, 107
Balliol, Edward, King of Scotland 74
Balliol, John, King of Scotland 20, 46
ballista *110*
'Bamburgh Beast' 21
Bamburgh Castle *10*, *11*, 16, **20–21**
Bankes, H.J.R. 61
Bankes, Sir John 61, 62
Bankes, Lady Mary 62
Bankes, Sir Ralph 61
barbican *11*
barmkins 14
Barons' Rebellion 32, 34
Beauchamp, Guy de, 10th Earl of Warwick 34
Beauchamp, Richard de, 13th Earl of Warwick 34
Beauchamp, Richard, Earl of Worcester 110
Beauchamp, Thomas de, 11th Earl of Warwick 34
Beaufort, Duke of 100
Beaufort, Henry Somerset, 5th Duke of 103
Beaufort, Margaret 116,

118
Beaumaris Castle *1*, 12, *12*, 98, **128–9**, 132
Beaumont (de Newburgh), Henry de, 1st Earl of Warwick 34
Bede, The Venerable 20
Bek, Bishop Anthony 22
Belleme, Robert de *60*
Berkeley Castle 16, **40–42**
Berkeley family 40, 42
Bertram, Master 134
Bigod, Roger III, Earl of Norfolk 106, 107
Birch, Colonel John 38
Bloet, Elizabeth 103
Bloet, Walter 103
Bodiam Castle 13, *13*, **56–8**
Bodley, Sir Josias 147
Bolbeck, Walter de 74
Boleyn, Anne 46, 48, 59, 116, 153
Boru, Brian, High King of Ireland 149
Bosanquet, Mrs Edmund 37
Bothwell, Francis Stewart, 5th Earl of 74
Bothwell, James Hepburn, 4th Earl of 76
Bothwell, Patrick Hepburn, Earl of 82
Bothwell Castle **82–3**
Bowl Hole 21
Braose, William de 100
Breac, Jan 95
Bren, Llywelyn 110
Breteuil, Roger de 106
Brooke, 2nd Lord 34
Brooke, Sir Fulke Greville, 1st Lord 34, 36
Brown, Lancelot 'Capability' 34
Brown, Robert, the Younger 97
Bruce, Edward 138, 147
Buccleugh, Duke of 74
Buckler, C.A. 59, 60
Bulkeley, Colonel Richard 128
Bunratty Castle 136, *137*, **145–6**
Burgh, Hubert de 54, 100, 102
Burgh, Robert de 52
Burgh, William de 138
Bute, 2nd Marquess of 84
Bute, 3rd Marquess of 84
Bute, John Crichton Stuart, 4th Marquess 110
Bute, John Patrick Crichton Stuart, 3rd Earl of 110
Butler, Arthur, 6th Marquess and 23rd Earl of Ormonde 152
Butler, James, 2nd Duke of Ormonde 152
Butler, James, 3rd Earl of Ormonde 152, 154
Butler, James, 3rd Marquess of Ormonde 152

Butler, James, 12th Earl of Ormonde 152
Butler, James, 19th Earl and 1st Marquess of Ormonde 152
Butler, James ('the Foreigner') 154, 155
Butler, Richard, 1st Earl of Glengall 154, 155
Butler, Richard, 2nd Earl of Glengall 154
Butler, Thomas, Lord Baron of Cahir 154
Butler, Walter, 3rd Duke of Ormonde 152
Byron, John Lord 124

Caerlaverock Castle *1*, *4*, 11, **71–3**
Caernarfon Castle 98, **124–7**, 132
Caerphilly Castle 12, *12*, 31, 98, **110–13**
Cahir Castle 6, **154–5**
Caledonian Canal 91
Canice (Cainaech), St 152
cannons 20, *84*
Cardinan, Isolda de 64
Cardinan, Robert de 64, 65
Carew, Sir George 148
Carlisle, Andrew de Harcla, Earl of 18
Carlisle Castle **18–19**
Carrickfergus Castle 136
Carter, Colonel John 130
Cashel, Rock of 136, **149–51**
Castell Carndochan 122
Castell y Bere 122
castle:
  definition 6–7
  types 6, 7–15, *8*, *10*, *12*, *13*, *14*
Castle Rising 8, 9, 11, **29–30**
Ceolwulf, King of Northumbria 25
Charles I 34, 43, 68, 77, 107, 128, 153
  statue *87*
Charles II 40, 43, 44, 59, 88
Charles, Prince of Wales 124
Charlie, Bonnie Prince 18, 19, 79
  waistcoat *95*
Charteris, Lady Margaret Butler 155
Charteris, Richard Butler 154
Chartist Movement 49
Chaworth, Payn de 114
Chepstow Castle 11, **106–109**, 153
Chester, Hugh d'Avranches, Earl of 124
Churchill, Winston *53*
Cinque Ports, Lord Warden of 55

Clare, Eleanor de 110
Clare, Gilbert de, II, Earl of Gloucester 12, 50, 110
Clare, Gilbert de, III 110
Clare, Gillbert FitzGilbert de, 1st Earl of Pemroke 116
Clare, Isabel de 106
Clare, Richard de (13th century) 112
Clare, Richard de 'Stongbow' 116, 136, 142, 152
Clare, Thomas de 145
Clarence, George Plantagenet, Duke of 34, 46
Clarke, John 25
Clavering Castle 8
Clinton, Geoffrey de 31
Clitherow, Elizabeth 56
Cobb, J.R. 116, 118
Comyn, Sir Alexander 90
Comyn, Elizabeth 37
Comyn, John 18
concentric castles 7, 11–12, 48, 110, 114, 121, 133–5
Conisbrough Castle **27–8**
Conway, 3rd Lord 130
Conway of Ragley, Edward, Lord 130
Conwy Castle 98, 99, 124, **130–132**
Corbeil, Archbishop William de 50
Corfe Castle 16, **61–3**
Cornwall, Edmund Plantagenet, Earl of 64
Courcy, John de 138–9
Covenanters 68, 70, 71, 73, 77, 88, 89, *89*, 90
Cowdray, Annie, 1st Viscountess 88
Crawford, Alexander Lindsay, Earl of 69
Crewe, Nathaniel, Bishop of Durham 20
Criccieth Castle 121
Crichton, James, 2nd Lord 82
Crichton, Sir William 69
Cromwell, Oliver *33*, 42, 62, 77, 103, 116, 134, 138, 154
Cromwell, Thomas 46
Crovan, Godred 96
Crown Jewels 46, 48
Cubitt, George, Lord Ashcombe 56
curtain walls 9, *9*, 11, *12*, 36, 46, *52*, *54*, *63*, 85, 108, 129, 142
Curzon, Lord 56

Dafydd ab Euian ab Einion 119
Dalyngrigge, Sir Edward 56, 57, 58
  crest *58*

Clare, Eleanor de 110
David I 18, 20, 22, 77
David II 14, 43, 77
Davies, Father William 128
Despenser, Hugh le 37, 106, 110, 113
Despenser, Isabel 110
Devereux, Robert, Earl of Essex 155
Din Eidyn 77
Dolbadarn Castle 122
Dolforwyn Castle 122
Dolwyddelan Castle 7, 98, **122–3**
Domesday Book 40, 56, 64
Donald II 88
Douglas, Archibald 68
Douglas, Archibald 'the Grim', 3rd Earl of 68, 82
Douglas, David 69
Douglas, James 69
Douglas, Sir James, 2nd Earl 68
Douglas, James, 9th Earl 70
Douglas, Sir William 74
Douglas, William, 1st Earl 74
Douglas, William, 6th Earl 69
Douglas, William, 8th Earl 69, 79
Dover Castle 8, 11, 16, **52–5**
Dubh, Iain 96–7
Dubris 53
Dudley, Lord Guilford 46
Dudley, John, Duke of Northumberland 31
Dudley, Robert, Earl of Leicester 31, 32, *33*
Duffus Castle 6
Dugdale, Sir William 31
Dun Iascaigh 154
Dunnottar Castle 14, **88–9**
Dunvegan Castle 14, 66, 84, **93–5**
Durobrivae 50
Durward, Alan 90

Earp, Thomas 59
Edgar, King 61
Edinburgh Castle 14, **77–8**
Edinburgh Military Tattoo *78*
Edmund, Duke of York 29
Edward I 12, 18, 38, 46, 48, 59, 71, 72, 74, 77, 79–80, 82, 90, 100, 110, 119, 122, 123, 124, 126, 127, 128, 130, 132, 133–4
Edward II 18, *27*, 29, *30*, 31, 34, 41, 110
  arms *18*
  statue *124*
Edward III 25, 27, 29, *30*, 43, 50, 51, 82, 88
Edward IV 27, 34, 37, 43, 45, 103
Edward V 46
Edward VI 31, 34

Edward VII 43, 124, 153
Edward VIII 43
Edward Balliol, King of Scotland 74
Edward, the Black Prince 29, 64
Edward of Caernarfon, Prince of Wales 124
Edward the Confessor 8
Edward the Elder 133
Edward the Martyr, King 61
Eilean Donan Castle 66, 67, **92–4**
Eleanor, Queen 124, 133
Elizabeth I 6, 31, 32, *33*, 46, 59, 61, 154, 155
Elizabeth II 44, 79
Elizabeth, Queen Mother 43, 55, 66, 86
English Civil War 27, 31, 34, 37, 38, *60*, 62, 88, 103, 109, 134
Eresby, Lord Willoughby de 122
Essex, Robert Devereux, Earl of 155
Ethelfleda 34
Ethelred, King 61
Eustace, Count of Boulogne 52
Ewloe Castle 122

Fairy Flag 96–7
Fitzalan, John, Lord of Clun and Oswestry 59
Fitzalan, Richard, 1st Earl of Arundel 59
Fitzalan-Howard, Edward William, 18th Duke of Norfolk 59
Fitzgerald, Colin 92
Fitzgerald, Gareth mor, 8th Earl of Kildare 140
Fitzgerald, Thomas ('Silken Thomas'), 10th Earl of Kildare 142
Fitzharding, Robert 40
Fitzharding, William 40
Fitzjohn, Eustace 20, 22
FitzOsbern, William, Earl of Hereford 40, 100, 106, 108–9
FitzRichard, Roger 25
FitzRoger, Robert 25
FitzTurstin, Baldwin 64
FitzWalter, Theobald 152
Fitzwarne, William 90
Flint Castle 130, 133
Forbes, Sir Alexander de 90
Forfar, Archibald Douglas, 1st Earl of 82
Forster, Claudius 20
Forster, Sir John 22
Framlingham Castle 11
Fuller, John 56

gatehouses *11*, *12*, 13
Gaveston, Piers 34
Geneville, Geoffrey de 142

George III 43
George V 153
George VI 86
Gibbons, Grinling 44
Giffard, John 34
Glamis, Patrick, 9th Lord 86
Glamis, Patrick Lyon, 1st Lord 86, 87
Glamis Castle 14, 66, 84, **86–7**
Glengall, Richard Butler, 1st Earl of 154, 155
Glengall, Richard Butler, 2nd Earl of 154
Gloriette, Corfe Castle *61*, 62
Gloucester, Gilbert de Clare II, Earl of 12, 50, 110
Gloucester, Humphrey, Duke of 116, 142
Glyndwr Rebellion 116
Godwin, Earl 40
Godwinson, Harold 43, 133
Goodrich Castle **37–9**
Gordon, George, 2nd Earl of Huntly 90
Gorm, Donald 92
Gort, 7th Viscount Lord 145
Gort, Viscount Lord (19th century) 147
Graham, Sir John 74
Grandison, Sir Otto de 124
Grant of Freuchie, John 91
Grant Highlanders 90
Grenville, Sir Richard 64
Greville, Francis, Earl of Warwick 34
Greville, Sir Fulke, 1st Lord Brooke 34, 36
Greville, Fulke (later Howard) 29
Grey, Henry, Earl of Kent 37
Grey, Lady Jane 31, 46
Grey, Lord, of Ruthin 122
Grey, Sir Ralph 25
Griffin, Admiral Thomas 37
Grosmont 102
Gruffydd ap Llywelyn 134
Grug, Rhys 114
Gurney, Sir Thomas 41
Gwilym ap Tudor 132

Hamlet 88
Harald Hardrada 96
Harcla, Andrew de, Earl of Carlisle 18
Harlech Castle 12, 98, **119–21**, 132, 140
Harold II 8, 16
Hatton, Sir Christopher 61
Henrietta Maria 52
Henry I 18, 19, 20, 50, 59, 61, 106, 114
Henry II 18, 20, 25, 37, 40, 43, 52, 54, 79, 100, 136, 142, 149, 152
Henry III 46–8, 50, 51, 102, 122

Henry IV 23, 25, 46
Henry V 25, 116, 142
Henry VI 20, 116
Henry VII 40, 45, 114, 116, 118
Henry VIII 6, 18, 19, 43, 45, 50, 59, 71, 145
Hepburn, James, 4th Earl of Bothwell 76
Hepburn, Patrick, Earl of Bothwell 74, 82
Herbert, Sir Walter 103
Herbert, William 37, 103
Herbert, Sir William 103
Hereford Castle 8
Hereford, William FitzOsbern, Earl of 40, 100, 106, 108–9
Hermitage Castle 66, **74–6**, 82, 146
Hess, Rudolf 46, 100
Holyroodhouse, Palace of 77
Honours of Scotland 78, 88
Hope-Taylor, Dr Brian 21
hornwork *112*, 113
Howard, Greville 30
Howard, Henry, 15th Duke of Norfolk 59
Howard, Henry, Duke of Norfolk (17th century) 29
Howard, Katherine 46, 48, 59
Howard, Philip 59
Howard, Thomas, 3rd Duke of Norfolk 29, 59
Howard, Thomas, 4th Duke of Norfolk 59
Hugh d'Avranches, Earl of Chester 124
Hulle (Howle) 37
Huntingdon, Henry, Earl of 20
Huntly, George Gordon, 2nd Earl of 90

Ida, King 20
Inchiquin, Murrogh O'Brien, Lord 154
Ireton, General Henry 147
Isabel, Queen of Scotland 50
Isabella, Queen 29, 30, 41, 59, 110, 113

Jackson, Sir Henry Mather 100
Jacobite Rising 19, 79, 92
Jakobs, Josef 46
James I (VI of Scotland) 20, 34, 43, 50, 74, 78, 79, 81, 86, 88, 114
statue *87*
James II of Scotland 69–70, 78, 79
James III of Scotland 77
James IV of Scotland 68, 74, 78, 80, 85, 91
James V of Scotland 79, 81, 85, 86

James VIII (Old Pretender) 86
James of St George 119, 120, 124, 128, 130, 132, 134
Joan, Queen 79
John, King 16, 22, 27, 37, 50, 51, 61, 61–2, 100, 138
John Balliol, King of Scotland 20, 46
John of Gaunt 31
Johnson, Dr Samuel 95
Jones, John Paul 138

keeps 11, *11*, 46, *47*, 82, *83*
cruciform 142, *143*, *144*
domed *116*, 117
hall- *108*, 109
keep-gatehouse 118, *118*
shell 9, 64–5
Keith, William, 4th Earl Marischal (William o' the Tower) 89
Keith, William, 7th Earl Marischal 88
Keith, Sir William, Great Marischal 88, 89
Kemeys, Sir Nicholas 106
Kenilworth Castle *4*, *11*, **31–3**, 110
Kenneth I Macalpin, King 79
Kent, Henry Grey, Earl of 37
Kidwelly Castle 12, 98, **114–15**
Kildare, Gareth mor Fitzgerald, 8th Earl of 140
Kildare, Thomas Fitzgerald ('Silken Thomas'), 10th Earl of 142
Kilkenny Castle 136, **152–3**
Kinghorne, Charles, 6th Earl 86
Kinghorne, John, 9th Earl 86
Kinghorne, Patrick Lyon, 1st Earl 86, 87
Kinghorne, Patrick Lyon, 3rd Earl 87
Knout (Knut), Sir Richard 74

Lacy, Hugh de, 1st Lord of Meath 142
Lacy, Hugh de, Earl of Ulster 138, 139
Lancaster, Edmund 'Crouchback', Earl of 100
Lancaster, Thomas Plantagenet, Earl of 27
Langton, Archbishop Stephen 50
Lauder, Sir Robert 90
Leicester, Robert Dudley, Earl of 31, 32, *33*
Leicester, Simon de Montfort, 6th Earl of 31, 50, 64

Lennox, Earl of 84
Leod, Prince 95
Lewis, Thomas 110
Lewknor, Sir Roger 56
Lewknor, Sir Thomas 56
Limerick Castle 9, 11, 136, **147–8**
Lindsay, Alexander, Earl of Crawford 69
Lindsay, sir James 86
Lindsay, William, Lord of the Byres 88
Lingen, Sir Henry 38
Llantilio 100, 102
Llwyd, Sir Gruffydd 119
Llywelyn ap Gruffydd 110, 113, 122, 123
Llywelyn ap Iorwerth (the Great) 114, 122, 123
Londinium 46
Longchamp, William 46
Louis, Prince, the Dauphin (later Louis VII) 43, 52
Lucan, Patrick Sarsfield 147
Luguvalium 18
Lyon, Sir John 86
Lyon, Patrick, 1st Earl of Kinghorne 86, 87
Lyon, Patrick, 3rd Earl of Kinghorne 87
Lysaght, D.R. 109

McCarthy, Cormac 149, 150–51
MacCrimmons 95
MacDonald, Alexander, Earl of Ross 90
MacDonald, John, Lord of the Isles 69
Macdonald of Lochalsh, Donald, Lord of the Isles 90
MacKenzie, John 92
MacKenzie, Kenneth 92
MacKenzie, William, 5th Earl of Seaforth 92
MacLellan, Sir Patrick 69
MacLeod, Alasdair Crotach 95, 96
MacLeod, John 95
MacLeod, Malcolm 95
MacLeod, Norman 95, 97
MacLeod, Reginald 95
MacNamaras 145, 146
MacRae, Donald 92
MacRae, Farquhar 92
MacRae-Gilstrap, Lt-Col. John 92
MacRaes, crest 92
Madog ap Llywelyn 119, 124, 128, 132
Magna Carta 40
Magnus Barefoot, King 84
Malby, Sir Nicholas 140, 141
Malcolm II of Scotland 86
Maltravers, Sir John 41
Mappestone, Godric de 37
March, Roger Mortimer, 1st Earl of 142
Maredudd ab Iuean 122
Margaret of Anjou, Queen

(wife of Henry VI) 20, 22, 119
Margaret, Queen (wife of Malcolm III) 77
Margaret Tudor, Queen 79
Marshal, William, Earl of Pembroke 37, 106, 108, 117, 152, 153
Marshal, William, Earl of Warwick 34
Marten, Henry 106, 107, *109*
Mary of Guise 81, 86
Mary I (Tudor) 31, 46
Mary, Queen of France 29
Mary, Queen of Scots 18, *18*, 19, 22, 66, 76, 77, 78, 79, 88, 96–7
Mathews, George 154
Matilda, Empress 59
Mauduit, William, Earl of Warwick 34
Maurice the Engineer 54
Maxwell, Sir Herbert de 71
Maxwell, John de (Muccnswell) 71
Maxwell, Lords 70, 71
Maxwell, Dame Margaret, Countess of Angus 82
Maxwell, Robert, 1st Earl of Nithsdale, Lord of Threave 68, *72*
May, Sir Hugh 44
Meath, Hugh de Lacy, 1st Lord of 142
Metfield, John de 128–9
military residences 6–7
mint 142, *147*
moats 13, *13*, 48, *85*, 100, 128, 135
Monroe, General Robert 138
Mons Meg 70, 77, 78
Montalt, Roger de 29
Montfort, Simon de, 6th Earl of Leicester 31, 50, 64
Montfort, Simon de, the Younger 31
Montgomery, Arnulf de 116
Montgomery, Roger de, Earl of Shrewsbury 59
Montrose, James Graham, Marquis of 88
Mor, Rory (Ruaridh) 95, 96
Moray, Andrew 82
Moray, Sir Andrew 82, 88
Moray, Joanna 82
Moray, Randolph, Earl of 92
Moray, Walter de 82
Moray, William 'the Rich' 82
More, Sir Thomas 48
Moreton, Thomas 40
Mortimer, Roger 41
Mortimer, Roger, 1st Earl of March 142
Mortimer, Roger de 32
motte-and-bailey castles 6, 134

motte castles 7, 9
Mowbray, Robert de 20
Mowbray, Thomas, Duke of Norfolk 106
Muchesney, Joan de 118
Muscegros, Robert de 145
Mytton, Major-General Thomas 119, 124, 128, 130

National War Museum of Scotland 78
Ness, Loch 90
Neville, Richard, Earl of Warwick 20, 25, 34, 103
Ninian, St 88
Nithsdale, Robert Maxwell, 1st Earl of 68, *72*
Norfolk, Edward William Fitzalan-Howard, 18th Duke of 59
Norfolk, Henry Howard, 15th Duke of 59
Norfolk, Henry Howard, Duke of (17th century) 29
Norfolk, Roger Bigod III, Earl of 82
Norfolk, Thomas Howard, 3rd Duke of 29, 59
Norfolk, Thomas Howard, 4th Duke of 59
Norfolk, Thomas Mowbray, Duke of 106
Norfolk Castle 11
Normandy, Robert, Duke of 61
Normans 7–11, 20, 138, 145, 147
Northumberland, Algernon Percy, 4th Duke of 24, 26
Northumberland, Henry Percy, 1st Earl of 22, 23, 25, 26
Northumberland, Henry Percy, 4th Earl of 25
Northumberland, Henry Percy, 8th Earl of 25
Northumberland, Sir Hugh Percy, 1st Duke of 24
Northumberland, John Dudley, Duke of 31
Northumberland, Ralph George Algernon Percy, 12th Duke of 24
Northumberland, Thomas Percy, 7th Earl of 25

O'Brien, Conor Na Cathrach, King of Thomond 154
O'Brien, Donal Mor 149
O'Brien, Donald (Domhnall), King of Thomond 152
O'Brien, Muircheartach, King 149
O'Brien, Murrogh, Lord Inchiquin 154
O'Briens, Earls of Desmond 147

O'Briens, Kings and Earls of Thomond 145, 146, 147
O'Connor, Hugh, King of Connaught 140
O'Connor, Rory, King of Connaught 142
Odo, Bishop of Bayeux 29, 50, 52
O'Donnells 97
Ogilvy, Lady 88
O'Kelly, Donogh 140
Orleans, Charles, Duke of 46
Ormonde, Arthur Butler, 6th Marquess and 23rd Earl 152
Ormonde, James Butler, 2nd Duke of 152
Ormonde, James Butler, 3rd Earl of 152, 154
Ormonde, James Butler, 3rd Marquess of 152
Ormonde, James Butler, 12th Earl of 152
Ormonde, James Butler, 19th Earl and 1st Marquess of 152
Ormonde, Walter Butler, 3rd Duke of 152
Osbert, King of Northumberland 25
Owain Glyndwr 106, 114, 119, 121, 122, 124, 128, 132, 133

Paris, Matthew 52
Patrick, St 149
Peasants' Revolt 46, 50
pele towers 15
Pembroke, Aymer de Valence, Earl of 38, 82
Pembroke, Gilbert FitzGilbert de Clare, 1st Earl 116
Pembroke, Henry Herbert, Earl of 110
Pembroke, Humphrey, Earl of 116, 142
Pembroke, William de Valence, Earl of 37, 38, 118
Pembroke, William Marshal, Earl of 37, 106, 108, 117, 152, 153
Pembroke Castle 98, 116–18, 153
Percy, 9th Earl 22
Percy, Algernon, 4th Duke of Northumberland 24,

26
Percy, Henry, 1st Lord 22
Percy, Henry, 2nd Earl of Northumberland 22
Percy, Henry, 4th Earl of Northumberland 25
Percy, Henry, 4th Lord, 1st Earl of Northumberland 22, 23, 25, 26
Percy, Henry, 8th Lord 22, 25
Percy, Henry 'Hotspur' 23, 25
Percy, Sir Hugh, 12th Lord, 1st Duke of Northumberland 22
Percy, Ralph George Algernon, 12th Duke of Northumberland 24
Percy, Thomas, 7th Earl of Northumberland 22, 25
Pevensey Castle 8, 16
pharos 53, 55
Philip Augustus, King 117
Philip of Worcester 154
Philippa, Queen 29
Philipps, Major General Sir Ivor 116, 118
Plantagenet, Edmund, Earl of Cornwall 64
Plantagenet, George, Duke of Clarence 34, 46
Plantagenet, Hamelin, 5th Earl of Warenne 27, 28
Plantagenet, Thomas, Earl of Lancaster 27
portcullis 36, 49, 58
Powell, Sir Nathaniel, 2nd Baronet Thanet 56
Preston, Lieutenant-General 140

quadrangular castles 7, 12–13, 13

Raglan Castle 98, 103–105
Raleigh, Sir Walter 46
Ralph of Grosmont 100, 102
Ramsay, Sir Alexander 74, 76
Ramsay, Vice-Admiral Bertrand 52, 53
Ramsay, Sir John 82
Randolph, sir Thomas 90
Restormel Castle 16, 64–5
Rhuddlan Castle 133–5
Rhys ap Gruffydd 114
Rhys ap Tewdwr 116

Richard, Duke of York 46
Richard I 79
Richard II 18, 20, 23, 29, 46, 50, 56, 124, 130
Richard III 18, 34, 56, 59, 116
Richard's Castle 8
ringwork and bailey castle 8
ringwork castles 7, 9, 136, 142, 147
Rinuccini, Archbishop 145
Roaring Meg 104
Robert I (the Bruce) 18, 25, 66, 71, 77, 79, 90, 92
Robert III of Scotland 84
Robert of Rhuddlan 133
Robertson, William 152
Roche, Thomas 116
Rochester Castle 5, 11, 50–51
Roger, Bishop of Salisbury 114
Rokeby, Sir Thomas 145
Romans 18, 46, 50, 52, 53, 110, 113, 124
Roscommon Castle 13, 140–41
Ross, Alexander MacDonald, Earl of 90
Rothesay Castle 84–5
Rowley-Conwy, Admiral 133
Ruthven, Master of 84

St Mary-in-Castro 53, 55
St Peter ad Vincula Church 46–8
Saxons 96
Schomberg, Frederick, Duke of 138
Scottish Wars of Independence 14, 72, 74, 79
Scrope, Richard 23, 25
Seaforth, William MacKenzie, 5th Earl of 92
Shakespeare, William 22, 86, 88
Sharpe, Dr John 20
Shrewsbury, Gilbert Talbot, 7th Earl of 37
Shrewsbury, John Talbot, 3rd Earl of 37
Shrewsbury, Roger de Montgomery, Earl of 59
Siddeley, Sir John Davenport 31
Somerset, Sir Charles,

Baron Herbert 103
Somerset, Edward, 2nd Marquess of Worcester 103, 104
Somerset, Edward, 4th Earl of Worcester 103
Somerset, Henry, 3rd Marquess of Worcester 103
Somerset, Henry, 5th Earl and 1st Marquess of Worcester 103
Somerset, William, 3rd Earl of Worcester 103, 105
Soulis family 74
Statute of Rhuddlan 133
Stephen, King 18, 20, 61, 100
Stephenson, Robert 130
Stewart, Francis, 5th Earl of Bothwell 74
Stewart, John 84
Stewart, Murdoch, 2nd Duke of Albany 71
Stewart, Robert 79
Stigand, Archbishop of Canterbury 29
Stirling Castle 79–81
Stone of Destiny 77, 78
stone enclosure castles 7, 9–11, 9, 10, 12, 14, 19, 20, 82, 89, 142
Strathmore, 9th Earl of 86
Strathmore, John, 10th Earl of 86
Stuart, John Patrick Crichton, 3rd Earl of Bute 110
Sussex, William d'Albini, Earl of 29, 59

Talbot, Gilbert, 7th Earl of Shrewsbury 37
Talbot, John, 3rd Earl of Shrewsbury 37
Telford, Thomas 130
Thanet, Sir John Tufton, Earl of 56
Threave Castle 4, 14, 68–70, 78
Throckmorton, Elizabeth 46
Tomen Castell 7, 122, 123
tower houses 7, 13–15, 14, 15, 66, 89, 90–91
Tower of London 11, 12, 16, 46–9
town walls 130, 132
Tracy, Sir Thomas de 64

Traitor's Gate 48
trebuchet 52, 110
Trim Castle 136, 142–4
Tudor, Edmund 116
Tudor, Jasper 110, 116
Tufton, Sir John, 2nd Earl of Thanet 56
Turner, Sir Llywelyn 124
Twthill 98, 133, 134, 135
Tyson (de Tesson), Gilbert 22

Ufford, Robert de 140
Ulster, Hugh de Lacy, Earl of 138, 139
Urquhart Castle 14, 15, 90–91

Valence, Aymer de, Earl of Pembroke 38, 82
Valence, William de, Earl of Pembroke 37, 38, 118
Vaughan, John 114
Verrio, Antonio 44
Vescy, Eustace de 22
Vescy, Isabel de 20
Vescy, Yvo de 22
Victoria, Queen 49, 79, 130
Vikings 84, 88, 145

Wallace, William 22, 79, 88
Walter of Exeter 71
Wardeux, Elizabeth 56
Warenne, Hamelin Plantagenet, 5th Earl of 27, 28
Warenne, Isabel de 27
Warkworth Castle 16, 25–6
Warren-Bulkeley, Thomas James 128
Warwick, Francis Greville, Earl of 34
Warwick, Guy de Beauchamp, 10th Earl of 34
Warwick, Richard Beauchamp, Earl of 110
Warwick, Richard de Beauchamp, 13th Earl of 34
Warwick, Richard Neville, Earl of 20, 25, 34, 103
Warwick, Thomas de Beauchamp, 11th Earl of 34
Warwick, Wiliam Mauduit, Earl of 34
Warwick, William

Marshal, Earl of 34
Warwick Castle 7, 9, 11, 16, 34–6
Webster, Sir Thomas 56
Weldon, Sir Anthony 50
wells 72, 102, 130
White Castle 98, 100–102
William I ('the Conqueror') (Duke William of Normandy) 7–8, 16, 36, 40, 43, 46, 52, 53–4, 59, 116
William I ('the Lion') of Scotland 18, 22, 25, 79, 90
William II 18, 20, 50
William III 34, 77, 138, 141, 147, 152, 153
William, Brother 74, 76
William ap Thomas, Sir 103
Williams, Mrs C. 122
Williams, John, Archbishop of York 130
Williams-Bulkeley, Sir Richard 128
Windlesore 43
windows:
arrow slit 11
mullioned 140
Windsor, Gilbert de 116
Windsor Castle 7, 22, 43–5, 110
wogan 117–18
Worcester, Edward Somerset, 2nd Marquess 103, 104
Worcester, Edward Somerset, 4th Earl 103
Worcester, Henry Somerset, 3rd Marquess 103
Worcester, Henry Somerset, 5th Earl and 1st Marquis 103
Worcester, Richard Beauchamp, Earl of 110
Worcester, William Somerset, 3rd Earl 103, 105
World Heritage Sites 12, 46, 49, 98, 119, 124, 128, 130, 132

York, Edmund, Duke of 29
York, Richard, Duke of 46

Zouche, William, Lord 110

# ACKNOWLEDGEMENTS

Seeing Llansteffan Castle silhouetted against the backdrop of the setting sun sparked an adventure for me, one that has seen me clambering over chunks of teetering masonry, slogging through muddy fields and fending off insects and hedgerows to reach some of the most amazing places. For years, it has been a dream to create a book showcasing castles in all their glory. I am grateful to New Holland Publishers for the opportunity to see that dream become reality.

I would like to thank the following people for their responsiveness, encouragement and suggestions: Jo Hemmings, Publishing Manager at New Holland, who first approached me with the proposal for writing this book. Kate Michell, Senior Editor at New Holland, for patiently — and promptly — answering a multitude of questions and providing support during the writing process. Harold K. Ewald, III, my brother, whose brain I picked when the writing challenged me, and whose unconditional support is a constant in my life. Marvin W. Hull, my husband, whose enthusiasm, insight and grasp of castle trivia have kept me on track. Tootsie, my faithful castle companion.